MY
BROTHER'S
Keeper

VANESSA HUNTER

My Brother's Keeper

©2022, Vanessa Hunter

vfhunter@gmail.com

Published by Anointed Fire House

Cover Design by: Anointed Fire House

Edited by: Anointed Fire House

ISBN: 978-1-955557-29-0

TABLE OF CONTENTS

My Brother's Keeper – From God's Perspective.............VII

Introduction...XI

Adam and Eve..1

Cain and Abel..17

Jacob and Esau...23

Rachel and Leah..33

Moses, Miriam and Aaron......................................47

Joshua and Caleb...57

Hophni and Phinehas..65

Tamar and Amnon..77

Saul and David...91

James and John...99

Peter and Andrew..109

Mary and Martha...121

The Prodigal Son..133

Mary and Joseph...147

Back to the Garden..165

Epilogue..CLXXXV

MY BROTHER'S KEEPER — FROM GOD'S PERSPECTIVE

When God created His God-man and placed him in the Garden, what was His ultimate plan for His creation? God wanted His creation to be made in His likeness and in His image. It was God's intent for His God-man to mirror in the Earth what he saw mirrored by God in the Garden. This wasn't an impossible task since God placed in His God-man the fullness of Himself. Everything the God-man needed to fulfill his assignment in the Earth was given to him by God. God also gave His God-man something he hadn't originally seen in the Garden: his soulmate; this was the one God pulled from the inside of him.

Is there any resemblance of God's original intent for His God-man in today's society? From then to now, how far has man fallen and what will it take to get man back to God's original intent? "My Brother's Keeper" was written to give us a window into how God deals with His creation through the lens of family relationships. My prayer is that as we walk through the different family dynamics with a biblical perspective in mind, we will find ourselves right back in the middle of God's original intent for His created man: the Garden.

On the surface, this can seem like a daunting task considering the time span from the Garden until now, however, it only took one act of disobedience to set the fall of man into motion, and it would take one act of God to rescue His God-man. The problem is the God-man must play an integral part in God's rescue plan, and according to my pastor, Apostle Bryan Meadows, when the God-man fell, he fell in dimensions. How could the God-man make his way back to his place of dominance and authority in his lifetime? Hence, our dilemma.

It's hard to imagine how easily the God-man was able to forget about his Creator. Surely, he must have known that the Creator's stern warnings were real and the punishment would be severe. I believe he must have given some thought to the fact that this act of disobedience would separate him from the only God he had ever known. Up until that point, there wasn't a reason for him to have experienced the Creator's correction, so I suppose he really didn't know what to expect. After having spent so much time in the presence of his Creator, it had to be devastating to find himself cast out of the Garden.

We know that God thought very highly of His God-man, after all, He made him in His image and His likeness. Even the angels inquired about how mindful God was concerning His God-man. The question one must ask is how mindful was the God-man of his Creator? Was the God-man so taken by the flesh of his flesh and the bone of his bones that he no longer desired the presence of his Creator? Maybe the God-man began to take his relationship with his Creator for granted, thinking that he would always have access to his Creator.

Like any good parent, I'm sure God longed to have his God-man back in His presence, walking with Him in the cool of the day. Being the God of the universe, He had already put into motion His plan to redeem His God-man back to Himself. In the meantime, His God-man would have to experience life from a lower dimension without all the provisions he once enjoyed in the presence of His Creator. What was once made available to him, he now had to toll for with his own strength. His one act of disobedience was costing him more than he could have imagined, and this was just the beginning.

It seems so unfair that the God-man's disobedience would have a negative effect on all the God-men that would come after him, and there was nothing he could do about it. What should have been Heaven on Earth had become separation from the Creator and subjugation to His enemy. Instead of ruling and reigning on Earth, the God-man had given up his right to rule and reign to another. So, the journey began, and families of the Earth had to survive the separation from the Creator until the plan of the Creator began to manifest in the Earth.

INTRODUCTION

After many years of being in the church and around the body of Christ, I have found navigating relationships in the church is an inevitable challenge that every believer must face. There are those who are radically saved from the moment they receive salvation, while there are others who had to wrestle with their flesh until they reached the full knowledge and understanding of what salvation was all about.

My salvation experience falls into the second category. I wrestled with my flesh until I came into the full knowledge and understanding of what salvation was all about. The beginning phase of my life as a Christian is one I would refer to as a carnal Christian. Even though I was drawn to Christ, there were so many underlying issues that needed to be dealt with that hindered me from fully embracing the love of God. My journey to maturity was met with many unexpected twists and turns.

Let us define some of the characteristics of a carnal Christian: The word carnal is translated from the Greek word sarkikos, which literally means fleshly.

There is a process we each must go through when we come into the body of Christ. Once we give our lives to Christ, the process of cleansing and renewal puts us on a path towards consecration and dedication to God. The truth of the matter is even those who are radically saved must also go through their process of consecration and dedication. It is important that we make space for those coming into the body of Christ to make the transition from babes in Christ to fully matured children of God.

One of the purposes of writing this book is to encourage the body of Christ and those who might find themselves struggling to get to their place of maturity in Christ. Also, for those who have made the transition from carnal Christian to fully mature children of God, to keep in mind that once you have overcome your flesh and your demons, you should be willing to help your brothers and sisters overcome their issues. My prayer is that you will find yourself in the pages of this book and trust God for your outcome. It is devastating when we hear of individuals who have left the church because they encountered another sister or brother in the middle of their process struggling with their personal issues. I believe we should lose the concept that those in the church should be perfect individuals. Let us give each other the opportunity to grow into who God has called us to be.

"Brethren, if a man be overtaken in a fault, ye which are spiritual, restore such an one in the spirit of meekness; considering thyself, lest thou also be tempted" (Galatians 6:1).

Many times, we are unaware of how the issues in our lives from childhood through adulthood, contribute to how we engage in relationships with both the males and females around us. Our ability to engage in healthy relationships should be one of the most important things we master as children of God. The gospel of Jesus Christ is all about human relationships.

My Brother's Keeper is an in-depth look into the different relationships in the Bible, to see what we can learn from the good and bad ones, how we can avoid the bad ones and how we can be changed by the good ones. If I were to ask you the question who taught you your relational skills, whose name would come to mind? The average person would have to admit that no one was intentional in grooming them when it came to relationships. We usually mimic those around us, whether they are healthy or unhealthy.

Therefore, we are going to take a deeper look into the differences between a carnal Christian and the mature Christian. Believe it or not, if we can only relate to others who are on the level of our places of trauma, more than likely, that trauma came from a relationship. We can become stunted in our growth because of traumatic situations and circumstances we have walked through. Unfortunately, we do not always make the connection between our behaviors and our relationships. For example, someone may find it difficult to speak up for themselves when they have been wronged by a brother or a sister; this is because when they were young, they were never allowed to speak up for themselves. They were constantly told by those in authority, "Be quiet and do what I said" or "Your opinion does not matter. Just do what you are told."

Let us turn our attention to the body of Christ, to the church house specifically, since a lot of trauma tends to surface in the church setting. If you have ever dealt with any type of hurt, pain, or shame, you will be triggered in a standard church setting. The church is the place where people come to get relief from past hurts and traumas. We would like to think that everyone in the church is there just to discover who they are, learn about God and have a community of people they can relate to. To a degree, this is correct. The truth of the matter is most believers must shed a lot of insecurities, hurts and offenses before they can begin their journeys of self-discovery.

The Word of God convicts us of our sins, but if we perceive the words spoken by those in leadership as a personal rebuke against us, we will be triggered by past hurts and traumas and allow what was meant to help us to offend us. We mentioned the carnal Christian earlier in the passage, but I would like to use a more common term: babes in Christ. When we are babes in Christ, it does not take much to offend us. Different people come into the church with different motives, such as to seek attention, to gain positions of leadership and influence, and sometimes, to grow their businesses, just to name a few.

Then again, we see those in the church who feel threatened by newcomers; they have always maintained a certain level of access and influence in their home churches, but now, they find themselves competing with others for the attention of the leaders. This is only their perception, of course, since true leaders are normally so busy that they do not have time to notice. Unfortunately, we see this a lot in the body of Christ. When we see this type of behavior, we know we are dealing with babes in Christ or occasionally, insecure Christians. If you are a mature believer in Christ, what is your responsibility toward the babes in Christ?

Hence, the birth of this book, "My Brother's Keeper." When God began to deal with me concerning the subject of this book, I was in a place of offense and really, I did not want to hear what He was asking of me at that time. My focus was on my own hurt and pain, and all I wanted to do was complain to God about the things I was dealing with. God has a way of disarming you in your place of self-pity. It is definitely true that many are the plans in a man's heart, but it is the Lord's plans that will ultimately prevail. If we want to walk in the best that God has for us, we must be willing to do things God's way. Humility will always lead the way when it comes to laying aside what we want and picking up what God wants for us.

My journey to wholeness began when God said, "Let Me use you in this," meaning let Me heal you and take what broke you and use it to help heal others. Although this was a really difficult time for me, it was exactly what I needed. One of the most humbling things in life that can happen to a child of God is when God says you are the man or the woman. I remember crying out to God about why He was allowing others to get away with certain things while holding me to a different standard.

I wanted God to deal with those who I felt were coming against me. I felt betrayed by God. How could He let them get away with hurting me and I just had to take it? I was heartbroken when instead of dealing with others, God began to point out things in my life that He wanted to deal with. I soon realized that there were things in my life, including a religious spirit, that God was not pleased with. I couldn't handle the thought that neither my attitude nor my mindset was pleasing to God. My perspective of how God deals with His children from that time forward began to change.

From that point forward, God began to teach me what Kingdom relationships were supposed to look like. God started transforming my life from the inside out. The process of healing was so freeing and liberating that all I wanted to do was please God.

When the time came to make the transition from a carnal Christian to a mature Christian, it was a difficult process for me. In order for me to truly lay aside the things that were hindering me from fully giving my life to Christ, I had to make drastic changes. Unfortunately, it is much easier to make outward changes than it is to make inward changes. It took me years to realize how different events from my past affected how I related to others. For example, divorce can leave you an emotional mess. If you do not take the time to get healed, you will find yourself trying to find emotional healing in others.

I have noticed that individuals who are wounded tend to attract other individuals who are wounded. One of the problems with these relationships is that once you start to heal, you find the things you once had in common are no longer there. One of the worst things you can do in your wounded state is to marry someone because of the hardships and pains you have in common. Most people think this will give them something to bond over when, in actuality, it makes them co-dependent on one another. If you plan to remain in your wounded state for the rest of your life, this may work. However, once we come to Christ, we will more than likely start the process of healing. This is, of course, once we begin to sit under the Word of God.

I would like to propose that after a new believer joins the church or a believer changes from one church to another church, the first thing that needs to happen is deliverance. This may seem a little drastic, but if we can deal with their wounds upfront, then the new believer will find it easier to integrate into the congregation. For believers who've joined from other churches, deliverance will help them to deal with any wounds from their previous churches and allow them to trust the members of the new churches they are now a part of. In the end, we will have a healthier congregation.

Truthfully speaking, this very seldom happens when we join a different church. As a result, we have a church full of individuals who are the walking wounded. This is where love comes into place with our brothers and sisters. We do not know all the things others have walked through prior to encountering us or how deep their wounds are. Therefore, we are forced to endure their growing pains until they come to their place of deliverance. How long this takes will be up to each individual person. For our part, we should consider how we would like for others to help us if we were the ones having difficulty getting our healing. I also believe those in leadership should have quarterly deliverance sessions, after all, there is no way we can carry the weight of ministry and not be affected by it.

The worst thing that can happen to the wounded individual is to encounter other wounded individuals who are still in the middle of their processes. The lack of love and patience needed to assist them in their healing processes can cause more trauma, rather than assist them in their healing. At some point, we must take a holistic approach when it comes to ministering to those in our churches. If we are honest, we have seen all types of mental illnesses come through the church and, as hard as we may try, there are some individuals who have fallen between the cracks.

> "There is a growing global mental health movement around the world today; and the global church is beginning to recognize mental health problems, which are the leading cause of disability worldwide— more disabling than such conditions as heart disease, stroke, or diabetes—as a major ministry priority.
> Mental health problems are usually the result of a combination of many factors, including family environment, biology, personality, spirituality, and challenging community contexts, including poverty

and violence. Increasingly, the impacts of traumatic events such as childhood abuse, interpersonal violence, or natural disasters are being recognized as major causes of mental health problems.

Research in the US shows that often pastors are the first persons a family calls when there is a mental health crisis. Yet, pastors are often reluctant or feel ill-equipped to speak about mental illness from the pulpit. Dr. Ed Stetzer, Executive Director of Wheaton College's Billy Graham Center, urges pastors to speak openly about mental health problems as one would about any other health issue and to educate their congregations. Stetzer has coined the phrase, 'sermons stop stigma'.

There are additional challenges. For example, the lack of consensus around appropriate terminology— mental health, emotional health, behavioral health, Christian wholeness—and around the relationship of mental health to spiritual causes, has hindered attempts at more collaboration. Another key issue is the role of culture and the critique that much of mental health is understood through the lens of Western assumptions."

Source: Turning the Church's Attention to Mental Health/Binding up the Brokenhearted, Gladys Mwiti and Bradford SmithThe Brokenhearted

I have learned to allow what God says in His Word concerning His ways versus our ways and His thoughts versus our thoughts to take root in my life. Just because I may feel a certain way about a situation, does not mean

God feels the same way, especially if it does not line up with His Word, even if I feel justified in my assessment.

"'For My thoughts are not your thoughts, nor are your ways My ways,' declares the LORD.' For *as* the heavens are higher than the Earth, So, are My ways higher than your ways. And My thoughts than your thoughts'" (Isaiah 55:8-9).

The premise behind this book "My Brother's Keeper" is we need one another to reach our destinies in Christ. For too long, the body of Christ has competed with one another, rather than embrace one another. If we are honest, each of us would have to admit that when we first gave our lives to Christ and joined the church, we came with our bags fully packed and weighted down. We were accustomed to carrying our baggage with us everywhere we went, and we dared anyone to try and take our burdens away from us. The weight of the baggage didn't matter. We would drag it, if necessary, to keep our baggage close by us.

I can imagine God watching us drag our bags from one place to another, desiring to relieve us of our loads and ease our burdens. His heart longing to strip us of the weight that kept us bent over in pain trying to carry the load all by ourselves. Jesus meant it when He said, "Come unto me, all ye that labour and are heavy laden, and I will give you rest. Take my yoke upon you and learn of me; for I am meek and lowly in heart: and ye shall find rest unto your souls" (Matthew 11:28-29).

I don't know about you, but I think I will take Jesus up on His offer. My prayer is that you will too. It's time for the body of Christ to read the Word of God, apply the Word of God, become the Word of God, and then reflect the Word of God. I believe the reason some of us have a difficult time fully committing our lives to Christ is because we have come to believe that it's too hard and we don't think we can do it. The truth of the matter is God never intended for us to do it alone. He has given us the Holy Spirit to lead us and guide us into all truth. But He has also given us the body of Christ and our brothers and sisters to help us get there.

God expects us to look out for each other. We are to be known for our love one for another. "Brethren, if a man be overtaken in a fault, ye which are spiritual, restore such an one in the spirit of meekness; considering thyself, lest thou also be tempted" (Galatians 6:1). The keywords are "you who are spiritual." This means that not everyone will have the capacity to restore a brother or sister in the spirit of meekness. While we are in the process of being formed into the image of Christ, we may stumble and fall, but God expects us to be there to pick one another up. This is not a license to practice sin, all the while expecting others to not hold you accountable. But this is to say that while you are working out your soul salvation, we are here to help one another along the way.

I am amazed, however, at how some individuals in the body of Christ feel the need to critique the lives of those around them without being invited to do so. For some reason, they have come to believe that they know what's best for others without taking the time to have a conversation with them. Never considering there may be things God has spoken to that individual about that they have no knowledge of. That level of immaturity seems to be commonplace in the body of Christ. The Bible teaches us that we should consider ourselves just in case we fall into the same type of temptation. I find it interesting how someone would allow a brother or a sister to bring gossip about another brother or sister and never once wonder if what's being said is true or not. But when they are the target of someone else's gossip, they don't understand how someone can be born again and talk about their brother or sister.

Somewhere along the way, their lives have become the standard for everyone else to measure up to. I'm sure in their minds, they are just trying to help their brothers and sisters to not miss out on their destinies and to fulfill their purposes in the Earth. All the same, I believe the body of Christ may have misunderstood some of the teachings of Jesus regarding purpose. It seems as if we all should dig deep within ourselves to discover the one thing God has placed on the inside of us to do and we must get to doing it. However, the Word of God is very clear that it is the ones who love God and that are called according to His purpose (not their own) who will do the will of God. "And we know that all things work together for good to them that love God, to them who are the called according to *his* purpose" (Roman 8:28). We can only find our true purpose when we seek the one Who gave us purpose. I don't know about you, but I believe God is more interested in His purpose manifesting in us than He is in ours manifesting.

When we understand God's purpose for our lives, we are no longer confused about how we should live our lives and what we should focus our attention on. One of the greatest things that can happen to us in this life is to walk in what God sent us here to do. Nothing can be more satisfying than that. If you really want to know your purpose in this life, spend time with the One who knew you before you were formed in your mother's womb.

In this book, we will walk through different relational scenarios from the Bible. My hope is you will realize there's nothing you have endured in this life that's not found in scripture. Not only are your issues found in scriptures, but the solutions are there as well. "There hath no temptation taken you, but such as is common to man: but God is faithful, who will not suffer you to be tempted above that ye are able; but will with the temptation also make a way to escape, that ye may be able to bear it" (1 Corinthians 10:13).

As we walk through the Bible, exploring different family dynamics, please keep in mind God is concerned about everything that concerns us. We know from the Word of God that the scriptures were written for our learning. Allow the scriptures to minister to your area of relational need. I believe the Word of God will answer the question, Am I my brother's keeper?

ADAM AND EVE

In Genesis 1:26, God said, "Let us make man in Our image, according to Our likeness," but it wasn't until Genesis 2:7 that He formed the man. "And the Lord God formed man of the dust of the ground and breathed into his nostrils the breath of life; and man became a living being." What was God's image and what was He like prior to making and forming man? In Genesis 1, we see the creative aspect of God. Every time God said "let there be," He saw what He said come to pass. What does this mean for us? It means that, like our Father God, we should say what He said and we should see like He saw. My question is what did man look like in Genesis 1:26? John 4:24 teaches us that "God is a Spirit and they that worship Him must worship Him in spirit and in truth." So, what man looked like in Genesis 1:26 is a creative spirit. By the time we get to Genesis 2:7, man is clothed in dust or Earth with the breath of God on the inside of him. It was the formed man that God placed in the Garden, and He placed everything in the Garden that man would ever need to sustain himself. God even placed a helper comparable to Adam on the inside of him. This is so that when the time came, a helper would be found for him.

In Genesis 2:24–25, God throws us a curve ball. "Therefore shall a man leave his father and his mother and shall cleave unto his wife: and they shall be one flesh. And they were both naked, the man and his wife, and were not ashamed." Wait, this begs the question— are the father and mother used as future references, or is this what happened to

Adam and Eve? Why would God mention father and mother at this time, and move past it without explanation? Did I miss something? It is important to note at this point that we don't hear anything about the serpent until a helper is made for Adam. We know that he was busy tending and keeping the Garden God planted for him, but what was it about Eve that caused the serpent to approach her? Obviously, the serpent must have been observing their movements and interactions, and found the perfect time to approach the Woman. The Woman was created as a helper comparable for Adam, but it appears she forgot why she was created. What happens when we forget why God sent us into the Earth? Instead of becoming the one who assists God in His work, we become the ones who hinder His work in the Earth.

Now, we begin to see the relationship between God and His man (Adam and the Woman) start to change. They no longer had access to the provisions that God placed in the Garden to sustain them, and the mist that previously went up from the Earth and watered the whole face of the ground was now cursed. Adam no longer referred to his wife as Woman; he now referred to her as Eve, mother of all living. I'm not sure if Adam and Eve understood how their lives were about to change, but they would soon find out. As my Apostle Bryan Meadows has taught, at that moment, Adam and Eve fell in dimensions, and now, instead of being in the image and likeness of God, they now ranked among the animals.

One can only imagine what it must have felt like for Adam to lose the intimacy he had with God, to be thrown out of the Garden of Eden, and to allow Satan to trick him out of what belonged to him. We understand why Satan did what he did when he tricked the Woman to eat from the Tree of the Knowledge of Good and Evil. The truth is he couldn't believe God would put anyone above him other than God Himself. When God made man in His image and according to His likeness, the man automatically became an enemy of Satan. At that point, he made it his mission to cause the man that God created to fall, thereby punishing God for the man He created.

"What is man, that thou art mindful of him? And the son of man, that thou visitest him? For thou hast made him a little lower than the angels, and hast crowned him with glory and honour. Thou madest him to have dominion over the works of thy hands; thou hast put all things under his feet: All sheep and oxen, yea, and the beasts of the field; The fowl of the air, and the fish of the sea, and whatsoever passeth through the paths of the seas. O Lord our Lord, how excellent is thy name in all the Earth!" (Psalm 8:4-9). We understand from historians that the actual translation should read a little lower than Elohim and not a little lower than the angels. This would explain the wrath Satan has toward the sons of God. In that one act of God making man into His image and likeness, Satan was reduced to a ministering spirit. Hebrews 1:13-14 reads, "But to which of the angels said he at any time, sit on my right hand, until I make thine enemies thy footstool? Are they not all ministering spirits, sent forth to minister for them who shall be heirs of salvation?" In Isaiah 14:13-14, we read, "For thou hast said in thine heart, I will ascend into heaven, I will exalt my throne above the stars of God: I will sit also upon the mount of the congregation, in the sides of the north: I will ascend above the heights of the clouds; I will be like the Most-High." That was Satan's desire all along, to be like the Most High God. Satan knew if he could exalt his throne above the stars of God, he could see prophetically what was coming into the Earth, and then he could intercept what God was sending. Daniel 7:25 reads, "And he shall speak *great* words against the Most-High and shall wear out the saints of the Most-High and think to change times and laws: and they shall be given into his hand until a time and times and the dividing of time."

When Adam and Eve fell while in the Garden, they gave Satan the authority and dominion that was given to them by God. So, now we begin to see Satan at work and prevail in the first family of God. God gave mankind the awesome privilege of stewarding His creation. We had the opportunity to make the Earth a reflection of Heaven. Jesus said, "Let Your will be done on Earth as it is in Heaven." I can't wait to see the Kingdom of Heaven displayed in the Earth to such a degree that nothing will be impossible to us. God's original intent for man to operate in His image and His likeness culminates in three words, "let there be!"

The story of Adam, Eve, Cain and Able is a constant reminder that there are no perfect families. Surely if the perfect family existed, it would have been the first family of Adam and Eve, along with their sons, Cain and Able. Just to be clear, God did not create an imperfect family. However, the perfect man and woman whom God created and placed as the head of the family fell short of their responsibility.

Seeing the situation in hindsight, it is difficult to comprehend how Eve could have believed God would withhold anything from her. I am sure if we examine our lives, there are things God has spoken over us that, when questioned, made us think or believe we got the short end of the stick. That our portion was not as great as someone else's portion, only to realize later that God was not finished revealing all that He had for us.

We are familiar with the dialogue between the serpent and Eve. Genesis 7:1-7 reads, "Now the serpent was more subtil than any beast of the field which the LORD God had made. And he said unto the woman, Yea, hath God said, Ye shall not eat of every tree of the garden? And the woman said unto the serpent, We may eat of the fruit of the trees of the garden: But of the fruit of the tree which *is* in the midst of the garden, God hath said, Ye shall not eat of it, neither shall ye touch it, lest ye die. And the serpent said unto the woman, Ye shall not surely die: For God doth know that in the day ye eat thereof, then your eyes shall be opened, and ye shall be as gods, knowing good and evil. And when the woman saw that the tree *was* good for food, and that it *was* pleasant to the eyes, and a tree to be desired to make *one* wise, she took of the fruit thereof, and did eat, and gave also unto her husband with her; and he did eat. And the eyes of them both were opened, and they knew that they *were* naked; and they sewed fig leaves together and made themselves aprons."

The truth of the matter is, Adam and Eve allowed a rebellious spirit referred to as Satan to cause them to disobey God, their Father, with one question. As a result of their disobedience, they set in motion a spirit of rebellion that would affect every family that would come behind them. We see this spirit of rebellion repeat itself in their son Cain.

Genesis 4: 3-11, "The day came when Cain brought a gift of the fruit of the ground to the Lord. But Abel brought a gift of the first-born of his flocks and of the fat parts. The Lord showed favor to Abel and his gift. But He had no respect for Cain and his gift. So, Cain became very angry, and his face became sad. Then the Lord said to Cain, 'Why are you angry? And why are you looking down? Will not your face be happy if you do well? If you do not do well, sin is waiting to destroy you. Its desire is to rule over you, but you must rule over it.' Cain told this to his brother Abel. And when they were in the field, Cain stood up against his brother Abel and killed him.
Then the Lord said to Cain, 'Where is Abel your brother?' And he said, 'I do not know. Am I my brother's keeper?' The Lord said, "What have you done? The voice of your brother's blood is crying to Me from the ground. Now you are cursed because of the ground, which has opened its mouth to receive your brother's blood from your hand.'"

From God's response to Cain's gift, we can ascertain that Cain understood his gift to God was not presented correctly. The question we must ask is why did Cain assume he could come before God on his own terms? We see the spirit of rebellion manifesting once again in the family of Adam and Eve, however, another spirit has now presented itself: murder. It would be unreasonable to believe that Cain's anger was triggered by this isolated incident. I believe Cain's behavior was a culmination of his daily life decisions and his attitude. Adam and Eve must have been heartbroken after losing one son at the hands of his own brother, but to have God send the other son away must have been unbearable. It was Adam and Eve's responsibility to make sure their sons understood the ways of God. Because of their rebellion towards God, they were kicked out of the Garden. Genesis 3:22-24 reads, "And the LORD God said, 'The man has now become like one of us, knowing good and evil. He must not be allowed to reach out his hand and take also from the tree of life and eat and live forever.' So the LORD God banished him from the Garden of Eden to work the ground from which he had been taken. After he drove the man out, he placed on the east side[1] of the Garden of Eden cherubim and a flaming sword flashing back and forth to guard the way to the tree of life." In the Garden, everything had been provided for Adam and Eve, but once they chose to disobey God, they had to deal with the consequences of their decisions.

Did Adam and Eve sit with their sons to explain the ways and processes of God? Were there discussions about why they could not enter the Garden, and what part they played in it? When parents ask their children, "Did I not train you better than that," the answer really is no. We get a clear picture of what training looks like when we consider what happens after someone starts a new job. Usually, the first thing management does is assign someone to train that individual by sitting with them to show them the company's systems and processes. Afterward, once they show them the system and processes, they trade seats. Now, the trainee must show the trainer they have grasped the concepts and are able to perform them. Once the trainer is convinced the trainee is now capable of functioning in his or her role, the trainer leaves the trainee to maneuver on their own.

On the other hand, parents usually tell their children go clean your room, go wash the dishes, or go wash your clothes, without taking the time to sit with them to show them how to perform the tasks correctly. Only later to become frustrated when the tasks are not performed to their standards. If we are honest, many of us serve a God we barely know, and the idea of getting to know Him seems unimaginable. Some believers are even envious of those who are intentional about following God with all their souls, hearts, and bodies. They see the blessings upon their lives that cause them to stand out among their brothers and sisters, and instead of being intentional about their own walks in Christ, they look for ways to assassinate the character of others. If they truly understood and knew the God they served, they would know we are all accepted in the beloved. However, with that acceptance comes responsibility.

God's punishment for Cain was more than he could bear. It is worth noting that Cain became concerned for his own life, while not once apologizing for taking his own brother's life. Cain wanted to know what would happen to him if someone found him. "And the Lord said to him, Therefore, whoever kills Cain, vengeance shall be taken on him sevenfold. And the Lord set a mark on Cain, lest anyone finding him should kill him" (Genesis 4:15).

How many of us, in our infancy, wanted God to avenge us of our adversaries? The only problem with this is that we may have served as adversaries to someone else. We can be our own worst enemies at times by refusing to submit our ways to God's ways. Cain had the opportunity to present his sacrifice according to God's requirements just like Abel, but he decided that he had a better way. If we are honest, we must admit that at times, we have prayed to God for specific blessings, but instead of waiting on God, we decide to help God out. Unfortunately, in our society, we have carried this mindset over into the church—that we want what we want when we want it.

We have allowed our disagreements with one another to cause us to hold grudges within the body of Christ. The Word of God says we are to be known by our love for one another. If we are truly honest, how many of us can say we love our brothers and sisters without excuses? God expects His sons and daughters to behave differently from those in the world. Our lives should be a living testimony of the goodness of God and His transformational power; it should provoke unbelievers to repentance and make them want to know our God. We have an obligation to not allow God to be despised in the eyes of the world. There should be nothing but honor for the house of God and His people. Let us be the living epistles read of all men that the Bible speaks about.

"Cain was upset and angry. *Why did God not accept his offering?* Sometimes our parent's choices may seem unfair. How then should we respond? The root of sibling rivalry is sometimes jealousy at how one child is treated vs. another.

God notices Cain's anger and tries to engage him in conversation. God does not ignore Cain's pain, but it is right there to help him. *Cain has an open door to God!* God has just spoken to him, yet Cain's anger seals off his ears and his heart.

When you are upset, do not be like Cain! When you feel you are being mistreated, go to God in prayer. Seek God's guidance and protection. Seek God's wisdom and guidance. Anger will not produce a good outcome that we desire.

When you feel you are treated poorly by your parents, go to them. Go to them with a heart that seeks to understand.

By exercising self-control and keeping your disagreement between your parents and you, and not acting out on your siblings, you will be more likely for your cause to be heard."

Source: Faithful Motherhood Focused on Raising a Faithful Family

It's time for the body of Christ to stand up and live out the true meaning of the Word of God. We can no longer afford to pick and choose which parts of the Word of God we are going to obey. God is calling His true ecclesia to arise and represent His Kingdom in the Earth. My prayer is that we will begin to walk in our dominion and authority to combat the wiles of the devil. Let's remember the fate of Cain. He wanted God to protect him when he was unwilling to protect his brother, Abel. The Word of God warns us to be not deceived; God is not mocked. Whatever a man sows, he will also reap. Trust me, the reaping is a whole lot worse than the actual sowing, and keep in mind that there are different levels of reaping. I remember when I began to get a revelation about sowing and reaping, I asked God when it was my time to reap what I had sown; please hold my hand until I get through it.

I believe God is ready to restore unto us everything the enemy has stolen from us, one of which is the family unit. We have allowed this world's system, Hollywood, and the music industry to redefine what's important, along with what we can live with and without. Because of a lack of knowledge concerning what Godly families were supposed to look like, we have allowed the enemy to trick us out of our marriages. It's time for parents to take their rightful places. Fathers can no longer abdicate their responsibilities to their wives and children, neither can women prefer the workplace over the household. We need single men to stop spreading their seeds as if they are trying to repopulate world without taking responsibility for the fruit of their loins. Also, it's time for single women to stop tricking men into having sex with them, ending up pregnant by someone they are not married to—men who are unwilling to take responsibility and provide for their children.

"Cain and Abel's sacrifices are both of the types we will see later in the temple. Yet, our sacrifices are not just physical but spiritual. Cain offered a sacrifice, but his heart was not right with God. How do we know this? If Cain's heart had been right with God, what should have been his first reaction after God did not accept his offering? His first reaction should have been sadness. *If his heart was genuinely seeking after God, his focus should have been on getting right with God as quickly as possible.*

God gives Cain instructions in verse 6. God encourages him that he can do better, but God also warns him that sin is "crouching at the door." (v.7) Cain is angry and frustrated. He chooses not to speak to God but to Abel.

God warned Cain that sin was a dangerous animal that was waiting to devour his prey, Cain. However, Cain was so consumed with anger that he did not listen. In his anger, he sinned. We must guard our hearts against sin and listen to God's counsel.

In his anger, Cain killed his brother. Killing Abel didn't solve Cain's problem. If Cain wanted to win God's favor, killing his brother was not the way to do it. Remember, this issue wasn't really between Abel and Cain, but between Cain and God.

Pride can be a destructive thing. When Cain's offering was not accepted, Cain's pride was hurt.

Sometimes we will throw away the thing that we most wanted when our hurt pride gets in the way. The purpose of the sacrifice was to build a deeper relationship with God. When Cain failed the first time, his pride was hurt. Instead of trying again, as God urged him to do, he instead decided he was going to cast it all away. Acting out in anger did not solve Cain's problem. Cain tried to lie to himself. He told himself the lie that the reason his offering was rejected was all Abel's fault. Then, after Cain killed Abel, he tried to lie to God and say that he knew nothing about it. The God who could see the real motives in Cain's heart when he came to sacrifice, was the same God that had seen Cain kill his brother. We cannot hide from God. God knows when we are treated unfairly. God also knows when we are treating others unfairly. God knows our true motives. God knows what our hearts are really struggling with. God knows our pain, our pride, our shame, and our brokenness. Just as God was quick to notice Cain's pain and to reach out to him, God is willing and ready to reach out to us. As Christians, we need to take our pain, anger, and hurt to God.

We don't need to put on a front and pretend that we are okay. God can handle our struggles. What if Cain had turned to God and listened? What If Cain had swallowed his pride and chosen humility rather than anger and pride? If Cain had listened to God, he would have still had a brother and his family. He would have had a home and work that was fruitful.

Sin has consequences. Sin breaks relationships. Sin breaks families.
Cain and Abel should have been lifelong partners and friends. All of that was destroyed by anger.
Abel was the gift of a friend to Cain from God, but Cain saw him as a rival for God's affections."
Source: Faithful Motherhood Focused on Raising a Faithful Family

It's important that parents get back to teaching their children the Word of God. There should be a regathering of the family around God's Word once again, led by fathers and mothers. It's time we take back the hearts and souls of our children; we can no longer sit back and allow the world's system to dictate their values, character, and morals. The enemy has usurped the authority of parents, causing parents to replace their time with their children with money and material things. The voices of parents have become almost null and void in the hearts of their children. They place more weight on the voices of today's athletes and entertainers than the voices of their parents.

Social media has become the most influential source of information in the lives of our children, and they have not been trained to know the difference between what is good and what is evil. We have allowed children ages six and up to determine whether they want to transition from a boy to a girl or from a girl to a boy, and some parents are going along with it. While parents slept, an enemy crept into our school systems and caused some of our kindergartners through high schoolers to believe that they are oppressors and others to believe they will always be the oppressed.

This is an abomination against the Word of God. We have allowed an anti-Christ spirit to go unchallenged in the lives of our children. If we are honest, it's hard for parents to combat the anti-Christ spirit in their children when they have not challenged the anti-Christ spirit in their own lives. God expects us to steward the gifts He placed in our care, and we will have to give an account of our stewardship. Jesus said suffer the little children to come unto me and forbid them not, for of such is the kingdom of God. Let's return to bringing the children back to God.

We should pay close attention to God's response to Cain. He is very much concerned with how we handle each other. The next time you are upset or angry with your brother or sister, consider the lives of Cain and Abel and allow God's words to resonate in your spirit. "If you do good, will you not be accepted?" So, if you want to know the answer to the question, "Am I my brother's keeper?" The answer is yes.

CAIN AND ABEL

"And the Lord said unto Cain, where is Abel thy brother? And he said, I know not: Am I my brother's keeper?"

"The first two brothers in the Bible were Cain and Abel. Cain was the oldest brother and Abel, the younger. Cain followed in his dad's footsteps and worked the land, and Abel was a shepherd. The Bible does not tell us what it was like being the first and only children. We do not know if Cain and Abel got along or if they were always fighting with one another.

One day, each of the brothers brought an offering to the Lord. As a farmer, Cain brought the first-fruits of his labor to offer to the Lord. Abel, as a shepherd, brought the firstborn of his flock. Even though they each offered a sacrifice to the Lord from the first of what their labors had produced, God saw the offering differently.

God chose Abel's offering and not Cain's offering. One brother found favor with God, and the other brother did not.

Children are not always treated precisely the same by their parents. Parents will have different expectations for older children than younger children. Parents may expect more based on a child's skills and experience.

When Cain did not win God's approval, his heart immediately blamed his brother. *Yet, Abel did not do anything wrong*. Abel raised his sheep and when the time was right brought a new lamb for the sacrifice.

Abel did not try to sabotage Cain's crops. Abel did not say anything to the Lord to lift up himself up and put his brother down.

They both could have received favor from the Lord. Just because Abel won favor did not mean that then Cain would not win favor.

When we are angry, it can be easy to lash out at those closest to us. When someone has made us upset, it can be easy to be mad at those around us.

We have to stop blaming others and direct our hearts back to God. We need to learn how to be happy for others, even if we do not win or do not receive what we want.

Cain was upset and angry. *Why did God not accept his offering?* Sometimes our parent's choices may seem unfair. How then should we respond? The root of sibling rivalry is sometimes jealousy at how one child is treated vs. another.

God notices Cain's anger and tries to engage him in conversation. God does not ignore Cain's pain, but He is right there to help him. *Cain has an open door to God!* God has just spoken to him, yet Cain's anger seals off his ears and his heart.

When you are upset, do not be like Cain! When you feel you are being mistreated, go to God in prayer. Seek God's guidance and protection. Seek God's wisdom and guidance. Anger will not produce a good outcome that we desire.

18

When you feel you are treated poorly by your parents, go to them. Go to them with a heart that seeks to understand.

By exercising self-control and keeping your disagreement between your parents and you, and not acting out on your siblings, you will be more likely for your cause to be heard."

Source: Faithful Motherhood Focused on Raising a Faithful Family

"And the Lord said to him, Therefore, whoever kills Cain, vengeance shall be taken on him sevenfold. And the Lord set a mark on Cain, lest anyone finding him should kill him" (Genesis 4:15).

"When God judged Cain for the murder of Abel, he became fearful for his life. The Bible speaks of God putting a mark on Cain to protect him from others.

God's mark of protection on Cain was to help provide for his safety. However, it did not prevent Cain from being attacked or murdered. The mark merely warned that anyone who killed Cain would himself suffer a worse death.

The fact that God had to put a mark on Cain suggests that the population was large enough that Cain needed to be singled out for protection. The text does not tell us what the mark was or that it was passed down to succeeding generations. As to what was the mark of Cain there have been a number of suggestions.

Certain Bible commentators have argued that the mark was merely a sign of confirmation that Cain would be protected from others. We are not told what sign God gave him, but whatever it was it calmed his fears for his life.

The phrase set a mark upon Cain (KJV) does not necessarily mean that there was some mark upon his person. The phrase more likely means a sign for him. This could mean that God gave some sign to appear for Cain's reassurance. Thus, the idea of a mark may mean some type of token or pledge. There are two other instances in the Old Testament where God gave similar signs to confirm His Word (Judges 6:36-40) and Elisha (2 Kings 2:9-12).

The Revised Version translates the phrase appointed as a sign for Cain. This indicates that whenever someone approached Cain some sign was given to deter that person from attacking. Though we are not told what this sign was, it protected Cain from those who wished to harm him.

None of these proposed solutions to the mark of Cain can be proven or disproven - we are simply not told what it was.

Scripture also tells us that in the future, God will mark His people for protection. For example, in the Book of Revelation we have an episode where people have a mark placed upon them. A special group of people, the 144,000, receives a mark from God that guarantees their protection. The Lord commanded:

Do not harm the Earth, the sea, or the trees till we have sealed the servants of God on their foreheads
Revelation   7:3.

Those not having the mark of God were not protected from the coming judgments.

In the Book of Revelation, we also find the mark of the beast. Satan always counterfeits the things of God. As God marked the 144,000 as a special people to be protected, Satan will mark all those who worship him with his name and number on their right hand and forehead. As is true with the mark placed on the 144,000 by God, the mark here speaks of ownership.

And he causes all, both small and great, rich, and poor, free and slave, to receive a mark on their right hand or on their foreheads Revelation 13:16.

Both of these marks were for the purpose of keeping the people safe who received the mark. Therefore, we can conclude that the mark of Cain fits other portions of Scripture where a mark is given as a sign of protection.

The mark of Cain was to help keep him from being physically harmed while he was a stranger and a vagabond. It did not guarantee his safety, it only promised a worse fate for those who harmed him. We cannot be certain whether the mark was an actual physical sign or something else. Marking humanity is something we find in the Book of Revelation. God marks his people with a sign on their foreheads. The Antichrist also marks his people with a sign on their forehead and right hand. In both instances, the marks indicated ownership and protection."

Source: Don Stewart Blue Letter Bible

JACOB AND ESAU

"When the time came for her to give birth, there were twin boys in her womb. The first to come out was red, and his whole body was like a hairy garment; so they named him Esau. After this, his brother came out, with his hand grasping Esau's heel; so he was named Jacob. Isaac was sixty years old when Rebekah gave birth to them."
Genesis 25: 24-26 NIV

We encounter the first set of twins in the Bible with Jacob and Esau. Their story is unique because we are given a glimpse of their lives inside the womb. I find it interesting how Rebekah was very much aware that her pregnancy was an unusual one, so much so that it caused her to inquire of the Lord regarding whom she was carrying.

Genesis 25: 21-28 reads, "Isaac prayed to the LORD on behalf of his wife, because she was childless. The LORD answered his prayer, and his wife Rebekah became pregnant. The babies jostled each other within her, and she said, 'Why is this happening to me?' So, she went to inquire of the LORD. The LORD said to her, 'Two nations are in your womb, and two peoples from within you will be separated; one people will be stronger than the other, and the older will serve the younger.

When the time came for her to give birth, there were twin boys in her womb. The first to come out was red, and his whole body was like a hairy garment; so they named him

Esau. After this, his brother came out, with his hand grasping Esau's heel; so he was named Jacob. Isaac was sixty years old when Rebekah gave birth to them.'

The boys grew up, and Esau became a skillful hunter, a man of the open country, while Jacob was content to stay at home among the tents. Isaac, who had a taste for wild game, loved Esau, but Rebekah loved Jacob."

It is incredible how Jacob wrestled with his brother, Esau, in the womb long before he wrestled with God. We can only imagine what it must have been like for Esau as the firstborn, growing up hearing the story of how his younger brother would one day rule over him.

How do you handle growing up knowing that both of you will carry nations within you, only to find out later that you will go in separate directions? It is hard to understand how we as parents can sometimes put a strain on our children's relationships. The Bible tells us that Rebekah loved Jacob and Isaac love Esau. Does that mean Rebekah tolerated Esau and Isaac tolerated Jacob? When we think about the relationship between the brothers, it is not difficult to understand how their family dynamics may have played a part in their dysfunction.

Genesis 25:27-34 states, "When the boys grew older, Esau became a good hunter, a man of the field. But Jacob was a man of peace, living in tents. Isaac showed favor to Esau, because he liked to eat the meat of the animals Esau killed. But Rebekah showed favor to Jacob. As Jacob was getting food ready one day, Esau came in from the field and was very hungry. Esau said to Jacob, 'Let me eat some of that red meat, for I am very hungry.' That is why his name was called Edom. But Jacob said, 'First, sell me your birth-right.' Esau said, 'See, I am about to die. So what good is my birth-right to me?' Jacob said, 'First give me your promise.' So, Esau promised, and sold his birth-right to Jacob. Then Jacob gave Esau bread and vegetables, and Esau ate and drank. Then Esau stood up and went on his way. So, Esau hated his birthright.

Genesis 27:2-34 reads, Isaac said, "I am now an old man and don't know the day of my death. Now then, get your equipment—your quiver and bow—and go out to the open country to hunt some wild game for me. Prepare me the kind of tasty food I like and bring it to me to eat, so that I may give you my blessing before I die.' Now Rebekah was listening as Isaac spoke to his son Esau. When Esau left for the open country to hunt game and bring it back, Rebekah said to her son Jacob, 'Look, I overheard your father say to your brother Esau, 'Bring me some game and prepare me some tasty food to eat, so that I may give you my blessing in the presence of the LORD before I die. Now, my son, listen carefully and do what I tell you: Go out to the flock and bring me two choice young goats, so I can prepare some tasty food for your father, just the way he likes it. Then take it to your father to eat, so that he may give you his blessing before he dies.' Jacob said to Rebekah his mother, 'But my brother Esau is a hairy man while I have smooth skin. What if my father touches me? I would appear to be tricking him and would bring down a curse on myself rather than a blessing.'

His mother said to him, 'My son, let the curse fall on me. Just do what I say, go and get them for me.' So he went and got them and brought them to his mother, and she prepared some tasty food, just the way his father liked it. Then Rebekah took the best clothes of Esau her older son, which she had in the house, and put them on her younger son Jacob. She also covered his hands and the smooth part of his neck with the goatskins. Then she handed to her son Jacob the tasty food and the bread she had made. He went to his father and said, 'My father.'
'Yes, my son,' he answered. 'Who is it?'
Jacob said to his father, 'I am Esau your firstborn. I have done as you told me. Please sit up and eat some of my game, so that you may give me your blessing.'
Isaac asked his son, 'How did you find it so quickly, my son?' "'The LORD your God gave me success,' he replied.
Then Isaac said to Jacob, 'Come near so I can touch you, my son, to know whether you really are my son Esau or not.' Jacob went close to his father Isaac, who touched him and said, 'The voice is the voice of Jacob, but the hands are the hands of Esau.' He did not recognize him, for his hands were hairy like those of his brother Esau; so, he proceeded to bless him. 'Are you really my son Esau?' he asked. 'I am,' he replied. Then he said, 'My son, bring me some of your game to eat, so that I may give you my blessing.' Jacob brought it to him, and he ate; and he brought some wine, and he drank. Then his father Isaac said to him, 'Come here, my son, and kiss me.' So he went to him and kissed him. When Isaac caught the smell of his clothes, he blessed him and said, 'Ah, the smell of my son is like the smell of a field that the LORD has blessed. May

God give you heaven's dew and Earth's richness— an abundance of grain and new wine. May nations serve you and peoples bow down to you. Be lord over your brothers, and may the sons of your mother bow down to you. May those who curse you be cursed and those who bless you be blessed.' After Isaac finished blessing him, and Jacob had scarcely left his father's presence, his brother Esau came in from hunting. He too prepared some tasty food and brought it to his father. Then he said to him, 'My father, please sit up and eat some of my game, so that you may give me your blessing.' His father Isaac asked him, 'Who are you?' 'I am your son,' he answered, 'your firstborn, Esau.' Isaac trembled violently and said, 'Who was it, then, that hunted game and brought it to me? I ate it just before you came, and I blessed him—and indeed he will be blessed!' When Esau heard his father's words, he burst out with a loud and bitter cry and said to his father, 'Bless me—me too, my father!'"

When we are forced to live with the consequences of our decisions, there is no one to blame but ourselves. How many of us will admit to not properly stewarding certain things in our lives, only to lose them and blame God for not warning us ahead of time? Can we admit to having a check in our spirit that we completely ignored because we wanted what we wanted without waiting on God's timing? Sometimes, our suffering can be traced back to a decision we made out of season. If we are honest with ourselves, the thing we thought we could not live without was the source of our suffering.

"Since Esau is the firstborn, it is difficult to imagine he did not understand the rights and privileges of the firstborn in his culture. Esau made a spur of moment decision based on a temporary situation, his situation was temporary, but his decision will affect him for the rest of his life. I am not sure if Esau realized in that moment that his contract with his brother was a binding contract, one that could not be reversed.

The right of possession into which the eldest son is born. The first son born to the father occupied a prominent place in the Hebrew family (Gen. xxvii. 19, xxxv. 23, xli. 51, xlix. 3; II Sam. iii. 2).

The first-born son took rank before his brothers and sisters (Gen. xxvi. 31, 32; xliii. 33). Usually, the father bequeathed to him the greater part of the inheritance, except when a favored wife succeeded in obtaining it for one of her sons (Gen. xxvii.; I Kings xi. 11-13). In early days the will of the father fixed the part of the chief heir, but the law of Deuteronomy demands for him a double portion of all the possessions and forbids favor being shown to a younger son (Deut. xxi. 15-17).

After the death of the father the first-born son was the head of the family; he had to provide for the widows of his father and for his unmarried sisters, since they ordinarily did not have any hereditary rights."

Source: Birthright: Morris Jastrow, Jr., B. Eerdmans, Marcus Jastrow, Louis Ginzberg

But what if our bad decision-making is a part of God's overall plan for our lives? The Word of God tells us that Jesus learned obedience through the things He suffered. I would say, if that is how Jesus learned obedience, we will more than likely learn obedience the same way. It could appear as if Jacob got away with deceiving his brother, but upon closer inspection, we see how Jacob suffered as a result, of his decision.

However, there is something we need to deal with concerning the prophetic word over both Jacob and Esau's lives. Rebekah was very much aware of the prophetic words over her sons' lives, but was it up to her to make those words come to pass? One can make the argument that since she heard the prophecy, she was obligated to make sure Jacob was in line to receive its fulfillment.

"Now Rebekah was listening as Isaac spoke to his son Esau. When Esau left for the open country to hunt game and bring it back, Rebekah said to her son Jacob, 'Look, I overheard your father say to your brother Esau, 'Bring me some game and prepare me some tasty food to eat, so that I may give you my blessing in the presence of the LORD before I die.' Now, my son, listen carefully and do what I tell you: Go out to the flock and bring me two choice young goats, so I can prepare some tasty food for your father, just the way he likes it. Then take it to your father to eat, so that he may give you his blessing before he dies.'
Jacob said to Rebekah his mother, 'But my brother Esau is a hairy man while I have smooth skin. What if my father

touches me? I would appear to be tricking him and would bring down a curse on myself rather than a blessing.'
His mother said to him, 'My son, let the curse fall on me. Just do what I say, go and get them for me.'" Genesis 27:5-13.

Jacob lived with the accusation that he was a trickster from the time he left his father's house but, in-actuality Rebekah was actually the trickster. She coerced her son into tricking his brother in order to steal his birthright. Could God have fulfilled His prophetic word without Rebekah's interference? I would like to believe so, but I am sure in the moment, Rebekah saw this as her last chance to make sure that Jacob would walk in the blessing.

Rebekah must have been pretty convinced that she was making the right decision to risk having a curse pronounced upon her life. As parents, it is important that we not get ahead of God's plan for our children's lives. We can cause undue hardship in their lives by allowing our impatience to override God's plan for them. As parents, how do we steward the lives of those whom God has entrusted unto us? The stewardship of Isaac and Rebekah was on display in the way they each favored one son over the other. I believe God intends for every parent to inquire of Him concerning the call and the purpose of their children's lives. I know there are parents who have been very intentional about bringing their children up in the fear and admonition of the Lord. Parents who didn't leave it up to the church to cover their children, but they prayed and interceded for them and made sure their children knew

God for themselves. Imagine how life could have been for us if we had parents who told us at a young age what God had called us to do in the Earth. It doesn't mean that all our trials, tribulations and traumas could have been avoided or eliminated. I believe if we knew who we were from a young age, we could have made different or better decisions that would have eliminated some of the traumas we endured in our lives.

One of the things parents should be mindful of in this day and time is, it is not wise to allow your children to be alone with any family or non-family members without vetting them first. The amount of damage that has happened to children because parents weren't discerning enough or didn't take the time to investigate those they left their children with is astonishing. The damage isn't always sexual, it can also be demonic or indoctrination into alternative lifestyles. This is not to blame parents, because most parents honestly trusted those who abused their children. But I'm sure Rebekah believed her son would be safe with Laban, after all, Laban is her brother. The scripture doesn't say anything about Rebekah visiting Jacob to check on him or to see how he was getting along, or if there was any communication between him and Rebekah regarding the woman he was about to marry. Jacob left home running for his life, neither his mother nor his father took the time to prepare him for the life he was about to embark upon. We can look at Jacob and say he reaped what he sowed and he got what he deserved. It wasn't Jacob's idea to take his brother's birthright; it was his mother's idea, and so it was her responsibility to make sure she covered him.

It took Jacob wrestling with God before he really understood who he was and what God was calling him to. Genesis 32:27-30 reads, "And he said unto him, What is thy name? And he said, Jacob. And he said, Thy name shall be called no more Jacob, but Israel: for as a prince hast thou power with God and with men, and hast prevailed. And Jacob asked him, and said, Tell me, I pray thee, thy name. And he said, Wherefore, is it that thou dost ask after my name? And he blessed him there." God asked Jacob his name so that he could make Jacob aware of how others saw him. Once Jacob was aware of how others saw him, God changed Jacob's name to Israel, meaning overcoming with God. Jacob now goes from trickster to overcomer.

From the Word of God, we know that in the end, Jacob comes into everything his father Isaac prayed over his life, but at a costly price. We also know that Esau was able to forgive his brother and they both reconciled, and the prophetic word was fulfilled. "Am I My Brother's Keeper?" Yes.

RACHEL AND LEAH

Let's look at Jacob through the eyes of his wives, Rachel and Leah; we know that the conflicts in their lives are a result of their father, Laban's unethical business practices. Laban's focus seemed to have been squarely on himself, to the point he used his daughters to enrich himself with wealth. It's not hard to understand why Laban would betray his daughter, Rachel. It was customary in those days to marry off the eldest daughter before marrying off the younger daughter. Maybe, he was trying to preserve the repetition of Leah. Why Jacob chose to work another seven years for someone he had contracted for doesn't seem logical. Once the marriage was consummated, they were married. The problem with it was he didn't give Jacob the opportunity to decide if that was something he wanted to do or not. What does it say about Jacob that he could get so drunk that he could lay with Leah all night and not notice that it wasn't Rachel he was lying with? He worked seven years for Rachel and didn't recognize that the one he was holding in his arms was not her. From Leah's standpoint, she had seven whole years to have Jacob all to herself, maybe by the time the seven years were up, Jacob would have come to love her.

We can understand how important children were to both Leah and Rachel, especially sons, but the fierce competition between them went way beyond just trying to give their husband children. At one point, they bribed each other just to sleep with their own husband and to have their handmaids sleep with him as well. God saw how Leah was despised in the eyes of Jacob, so He opened Leah's womb and allowed her to birth children to Jacob. Leah gave birth to three sons, and she thought within herself that surely her husband would come and make his home with her, after all, Rachel was barren and had not given birth to any children. Rachel, being the one that Jacob loved, found it difficult to accept that she was barren while Leah was giving Jacob child after child. It appeared that, at some point, they stopped wanting to please Jacob; the focus now was on which one could have the most children. Rachel tried to force Jacob to give her children, which caused him to become angry with her.

I wonder how much the sisters themselves thought about the part their father played in all of this. What if their father had kept his word? Rachel and Jacob could be happily married by now, whether they had children or not! Had not Leah been forced to go in and lay with Jacob, maybe she could have found someone to love her the way Jacob loved Rachel. What should have been a time of rejoicing for Rachel was ruined by her father. This event divided two sisters who should have been loving one another. Only Laban can truly say what his true intentions were when he switched Leah for Rachel, but whatever his intentions were, he appears to be very selfish. What do you do when it's your own father who betrays you, and doesn't bother to consider how his decisions have affected you and your sister's life?

"So Jacob went into Rachel also, and he loved Rachel more than Leah, and served Laban for another seven years." Genesis 29:30 (ESV)

We remember Jacob, the one who talked his brother out of his birthright. However, this time, we find Jacob among his mother's family. Rebekah sent Jacob away to live with her brother, Laban, in order to protect him from Esau, his brother. The story of Rachel and Leah is one that we have seen played out throughout many generations among women. However, in the law of the Jews, God made special provisions for his daughters.

Genesis 29: 1-28 reads, "Then Jacob went on his journey and came to the land of the people of the east. As he looked, he saw a well in the field, and behold, three flocks of sheep lying beside it, for out of that well the flocks were watered. The stone on the well's mouth was large, and when all the flocks were gathered there, the shepherds would roll the stone from the mouth of the well and water the sheep and put the stone back in its place over the mouth of the well. Jacob said to them, 'My brothers, where do you come from?' They said, 'We are from Haran.' He said to them, 'Do you know Laban the son of Nahor?' They said, 'We know him.' He said to them, 'Is it well with him?' They said, 'It is well; and see, Rachel his daughter is coming with the sheep!' He said, 'Behold, it is still high day; it is not time for the livestock to be gathered together. Water the sheep and go, pasture them.' But they said, 'We cannot until all the flocks are gathered together, and the stone is rolled from the mouth of the well; then we water the sheep.' While he was still speaking with them, Rachel came with her father's sheep, for she was a shepherdess. Now as soon as Jacob saw Rachel the daughter of Laban his mother's brother, and the sheep of Laban his mother's brother, Jacob came near and rolled the stone from the well's mouth and watered the flock of Laban his mother's brother. Then Jacob kissed Rachel and wept aloud. And Jacob told Rachel that he was her father's kinsman, and that he was Rebekah's son, and she ran and told her father. As soon as Laban heard the news about Jacob, his sister's son, he ran to meet him and embraced him and kissed him and brought him to his house. Jacob told Laban all these things, and Laban said to him, 'Surely you are my bone and my flesh!' And he stayed with him a month. Then Laban said to Jacob, 'Because you are my kinsman, should you therefore serve me for nothing? Tell me, what shall your wages be?' Now Laban had two daughters. The name of the older was Leah, and the name of the younger was Rachel. Leah's eyes were weak, but Rachel was beautiful in form and appearance. Jacob loved Rachel. And he said, 'I will serve you seven years for your younger daughter Rachel.' Laban said, 'It is better that I give her to you than that I should give her to any other man; stay with me.' So Jacob served seven years for Rachel, and they seemed to him but a few days because of the love he had for her. Then Jacob said to Laban, 'Give me my wife that I may go in to her, for my time is completed.' So Laban gathered together, all the people of the place and made a feast. But in the evening, he took his daughter Leah and brought her to Jacob, and he went in to her. (Laban gave his female servant Zilpah to his daughter Leah to be her servant.) And in the morning, behold, it was Leah! And Jacob said to Laban, 'What is this you have done to me? Did I not serve with you for Rachel? Why then have you deceived me?' Laban said, 'It is not so done in our country, to give the younger before the firstborn. Complete the week of this one, and we will give you the other also in return for serving me another seven years.' Jacob did so and completed her week. Then Laban gave him his daughter Rachel to be his wife."

According to the customs of the Jews, Laban could have allowed Rachel to marry Jacob without forcing him to marry Leah first. This speaks to the character of Laban. One could make the argument that it runs in the family, after all, it was Rebekah who'd convinced Jacob to trick his brother, Esau. Jacob's love for Rachel had to be strong for him to willingly work for another seven years to marry her.

> "In the customs of the Jews, it was disrespectful for the younger sister to marry before the elder. However, this law is not necessarily, but only a custom.
> The She'arim Metzuyanim Ba-Halakhah (145:39) quotes the Maharsham (Responsa, vol. 3 no. 136) as saying that this is merely a matter of proper conduct (derekh eretz) and not law. It is proper to allow an older sibling to marry first. However, when there is a real personal need, we can set this aside because it is not halakhah. Indeed, while an older sibling might resent a younger sibling who marries first, after a few years the hurt feelings might be strengthened on the other side. A younger sibling

who has to wait quietly for years as friends marry, unable to proceed because of an older sibling's challenges, may grow resentful as well. Because this is not law, it can be set aside to avoid pain.

Rav Yehoshua Leib Graubart (*Chavalim Ba-Ne'imim*, vol. 3 no. 78) goes further. He explains that this rule is the baseline practice for a parent marrying off children without preference — start with the oldest. Similarly, if a suitor arrives at the door and wants to marry one of the sisters, the older has the first right of refusal. Likewise, if a woman wants to marry into a family of two sons, the older son takes precedence. But if a suitable mate is found for the younger sibling faster, there is no need to wait for the older before marrying because marriage is a mitzvah (a good deed done from religious duty)."

Source:Torah Musings

We can only imagine Leah's disappointment when she learned that she was not the one Jacob wanted to marry, but her father forced Jacob to marry her without his consent. After all, she was referred to as having lazy eyes, while Rachel was referred to as beautiful in form and appearance. Surely, she must have heard the conversations within the camp regarding Rachel and Jacob. Perhaps, she thought this was the only opportunity she would have to marry and allowed herself to believe he would learn to love her. What is clear is that Leah loved Jacob and wanted to be his wife.

Genesis 29:31-35 reads, "And when the Lord saw that Leah was hated, he opened her womb: but Rachel was barren. And Leah conceived, and bare a son, and she called his name Reuben: for she said, Surely the Lord hath looked upon my affliction; now therefore my husband will love me. And she conceived again, and bare a son; and said, Because the Lord hath heard I was hated, he hath therefore given me this son also: and she called his name Simeon. And she conceived again, and bare a son; and said, Now, this time will my husband be joined unto me, because I have born him three sons: therefore, was his name called Levi. And she conceived again, and bare a son: and she said, Now, will I praise the Lord: therefore, she called his name Judah; and left bearing."

It is difficult to think of Leah trying so hard to please someone whom she feels hates her. We see this today in our society, women who desperately want to be married and are willing to live a life of misery just to say they have a husband. Please know you do not have to sell yourself short trying to force someone to love you. Trust God with every area of your life and wait patiently on Him. I promise you will spare yourself years of pain and disappointment by doing so.

Rachel and Jacob spent seven years planning their wedding, and when the time finally came, her father substituted her with her sister. Resentment towards her father and sister must have swelled up inside of her. Rachel knew Jacob loved her from the first day they'd met. Rachel had to deal with the fact that Jacob was married to both her and her sister.

Genesis 30:1-8 states, "And when Rachel saw that she bare Jacob no children, Rachel envied her sister; and said unto Jacob, give me children, or else I die. And Jacob's anger was kindled against Rachel: and he said, Am I in God's stead, who hath withheld from thee the fruit of the womb? And she said, Behold, my maid Bilhah, go in unto her; and she shall bear upon my knees, that I may also have children by her. And she gave him Bilhah her handmaid to wife: and Jacob went in unto her. And Bilhah conceived, and bare Jacob a son. And Rachel said, God hath judged me, and hath also heard my voice, and hath given me a son: therefore, called she his name Dan. And Bilhah Rachel's maid conceived again, and bare Jacob a second son. And Rachel said, with great wrestlings have I wrestled with my sister, and I have prevailed: and she called his name Naphtali."

Competition among sisters is somewhat common in our society today, but at the same time, very tragic. The thought that two souls can emerge from the same womb but not share a common love and bond for each other must be addressed. Rachel and Leah felt the need to compete with each other to find favor in the eyes of Jacob. In Jacob's defense, this is not what he had in mind when he'd asked to marry Rachel. His intent was only towards Rachel.

How does this apply to those of us in the house of God? Competition is just as strong among those in the church as it is in the world. I believe we often take the practices from the world and bring them into the church. We are aware that there is such a thing as healthy competition, but that is rarely seen in practice. There appears to be this need to outdo, to outshine, and to outpace others. What if, instead of competing with one another, we are intentional about helping each other see our own greatness and giftedness?

We see Laban's questionable character in the way he handled the marrying of his daughters to Jacob. But Laban's business dealings with Jacob were just as corrupt. I do not want to lose sight of the blessing Jacob received from his father, Isaac. Although Jacob deceived his father into pronouncing the blessing upon him instead of his brother, Esau, the blessing could not be reversed, so the blessing belonged to Jacob.

I believe it was his father's blessing that sustained Jacob in Laban's house. Upon closer inspection, we see Laban committing the same deception towards Jacob that Jacob committed upon his brother, Esau. He tricked Jacob into thinking he was marrying Rachel when, in actuality, he was marrying Leah. At some point, Jacob began to realize that his father-in-law was not an honest man.

Finally, Jacob decided to take his family and all his goods and leave Laban's house. This was after consulting with his wives and informing them that it was time to go. Jacob decided to leave without consulting Laban for fear he might restrain him from leaving. When Laban found out that Jacob had left, he immediately chased after them. Apparently, Rachel took one of Laban's gods and didn't tell anyone. I'm not sure why Rachel thought they needed her father's idols, but seemingly, one thing was very clear—he and Jacob did not serve the same god. Also, we see Rachel exhibiting some of her father's traits by taking his idols. It's interesting how Laban accused Jacob of being deceitful, when he himself had been deceitful towards Jacob the entire time Jacob was in his house. Laban checked the entire caravan looking for his idols. Rachel's one act of dishonor towards her father could have cost Jacob his life.

The Word of God is clear that we will reap what we have sown. From the time Jacob stole his brother's birthright and fled to his uncle Laban's house, until the time he left Laban's house, we see this principle at work. I know God looks on His children with compassion, because when we are still in this phase of our lives, we are still children, and He longs to see the day His principles begin to take hold in our lives. Reaping and sowing is a Kingdom principle. If we take the time to sow right things, we will also reap right things. Had Laban done the right and honorable thing by Jacob, when it came time to leave, Jacob would have made sure he'd honored his father-in law with part of his harvest. It is important that we not only know the Word of God, but we must also know His principles and how to apply them.

As Jacob made his journey towards home with his wives and children in tow, I'm sure the thought of his brother must have crossed his mind several times. Would Esau seek revenge? Would he try to kill him and his family? The truth is, Jacob didn't know what to expect or what would be waiting for him once he encountered Esau. One thing is certain—in all his pondering, he was mentally worn out and needed to go to sleep.

I believe that as Jacob slept, God let him know he was not returning as the same person he had been when he'd left. God had to help Jacob see he had become the person that he was destined to be, and that the prophetic word over his life was coming to pass. In his distress and desperation, Jacob was forced to go after God with everything that was within him, and he wouldn't take no for an answer. Jacob had learned to inquire of God and not take matters into his own hands.

At this point, although Jacob didn't know what to expect, he knew he had to continue his journey towards home. However, he chose to be very strategic in his approach. Based on how Jacob split his family into groups to go out before him, testing whether his brother would try to attack them or not, said a lot about where Jacob was in his deliverance process. Maybe Jacob needed to wrestle with God just a little bit more until his focus wasn't just on his own safety, but on the safety of his entire family.

We can only imagine how his concubines and their children must have felt knowing Jacob was willing to make them the first line of defense. Leah and her children were the next wave in the line of defense to protect Jacob. If Leah didn't know before, she knew now exactly where she and her children stood in Jacob's heart. It wasn't bad enough that she would always be second to her sister when it came to the affections of her husband, but the worst part was that he was willing to let her lose her life and the lives of her children to save himself and Rachel.

I believe God had mercy and compassion towards Leah and the other concubines and their children. Leah did nothing to warrant any of the hardships and pain she'd experienced at the hands of Jacob and her father. She had no say in the choices that were made on her behalf. Even with all the sons God allowed her to birth for Jacob, she couldn't win the affection of her husband. In all honesty, it was her father's greed that placed her in the middle of all the chaos. When we look back on Rebekah and look at her brother, Laban, it seems that being a supplanter (one who wrongfully or illegally seizes and holds the place of another) runs in the family.

We know that by the time Jacob finally saw his brother, all had been forgiven, after all, Esau's life had been just as fruitful as Jacob's life. This means that they were witnessing and enjoying the total fulfillment of the prophetic words concerning them, although it didn't look anything like they imagined.

"And Jacob was left alone; and there wrestled a man with him until the breaking of the day. And when he saw that he prevailed not against him, he touched the hollow of his thigh; and the hollow of Jacob's thigh was out of joint, as he wrestled with him. And he said, Let me go, for the day breaketh. And he said, I will not let thee go, except thoubless me. And he said unto him, What *is* thy name? And he said, Jacob. And he said, Thy name shall be called no more Jacob, but Israel: for as a prince hast thou power with God and with men, and hast prevailed."

"There is an interesting account in the book of Genesis that you've probably heard of but don't completely understand. It's found in Genesis 32:24, which says, "And Jacob was left alone. And a man wrestled with him until the breaking of the day."
Some have interpreted this as Jacob wrestling with an angel of God. Others say that Jacob wrestled with God Himself. Whether Jacob wrestled with God or a representative of God literally or in a spiritual sense, we can learn a thing or two about the thought of wrestling with God.
We all might have felt at some point that we were wrestling with God. Maybe you were (or are) wrestling with Him for healing, a breakthrough, or a restored relationship. Many times, God allows us to wrestle with Him for certain reasons. Let us look, into why God let Jacob wrestle with Him and how we can apply these reasons to our own wrestling matches with God.
Wrestling Is Not Rebellion but A Pursuit
Verse 26 gives us the reason why Jacob wrestled with God or His angel. It says, "Then he said, 'Let me go, for the day has broken.' But Jacob said, 'I will not let you go unless you bless me.'" Jacob wasn't

wrestling to keep or push God away. Instead, He was wrestling to keep God with Him."
Source: ChristianToday.com by Patrick Mabilog

We know that God remembered Rachel and eventually opened her womb. She gave birth to a son and called his name Joseph, meaning God has taken away my reproach. On the way to Bethlehem, Rachel gave birth to her second son, and she called him Ben-Oni, meaning son of my pain. However, Jacob renamed his son's name to Benjamin, meaning the son of my right hand. Sadly, Rachel died while giving birth to Benjamin. If we take a closer look at Rachel's life, although she was preferred over Leah, she also suffered more than Leah. While at first glance, it appeared that Leah got the short end of the stick, I would have to say it was Rachel who struggled through a lot of heartache and disappointment. It seems as if Leah finally got her heart's desire—no more competing for her husband's affection. When you see the dynamics of Jacob's family, you can't help but thank God for your family.

Jacob finally decided it was time to take his wives and children and leave Laban's house. Regrettably, Laban would not allow him to leave so easily. Did Jacob come to love Leah, and did Leah accept her place and role in Jacob's life? I am sure that over time, Leah made peace within herself, with her sister and with Jacob, realizing that even though she was not his first choice, she was still his wife. "Am I my brother's keeper?" Yes.

MOSES, MIRIAM AND AARON

The family of Miriam, Aaron and Moses is not as uncommon as you may think. We know that Moses was the third child born to his parents, and during the time of his birth, Pharaoh had a directive—he commanded that every male child born in Egypt was to be cast into the river. The Word of God tells us that his mother saw something special about Moses and decided to hide him. Everything about Moses' life appeared to be prophetic, from Pharaoh's daughter rescuing him from the river to his mother being commissioned to nurse him until Pharaoh's daughter was ready to bring him into the palace. This means that Aaron and Miriam spent time with Moses before he was officially raised by Pharaoh's daughter as her son. Although Aaron and Miriam knew him as their brother, Moses was too young to remember his brother and sister before leaving to live in the palace.

Most of us are familiar with a family member who was raised by another family member, and depending on their age at the time, that family member raised them as if they were their own. It's not until years later that they found out that the family member raising them was not their natural parent. Usually, the family's secrets are revealed, and the child ends up confused and hurt because they felt betrayed by the parent. The next question is typically—who are my parents? Usually, under these circumstances, the child finds it difficult to trust that parent, since there may be other things that the parent hasn't been truthful about. Naturally, if the parent is open and honest with the child, the easier it is for the child to appreciate the sacrifice the parent made on his or her behalf.

Sometimes,God's plan is to get you in an environment that is more conducive for the calling on your life. We may not always understand the manifold wisdom of God, but in time, we will come to realize that God was protecting us all along. On the other hand, we know that not all displaced children end up in good environments. There are some children who end up in abusive situations, and for them, it can take almost a lifetime to get through the traumas they endured during that season. This doesn't mean that there is no hope for them, it just means it's going to take God to intervene on their behalves. Thankfully, He knows how to bring the right people across their paths.

Like Moses, there may come a season when God will send you away from your family, friends, or familiar places to remove and work out the issues in your life. After this, He may turn around and send you back to help deliver them. There is nothing you can do or go through that will keep God from using you. God is more committed to you getting to your destiny than you are. Moses had to allow God to make him an instrument in His hand. Moses was to God what the staff was to Moses—an extension of Himself.

"Has the LORD spoken only through Moses?" they asked. "Hasn't he also spoken through us?" And the LORD heard this.
Numbers 12:1–15 (NIV)

48

Let's talk about rivalry among siblings. Any family that consists of more than one child has more than likely experienced sibling rivalry. For the most part, the interactions are fun and healthy, but occasionally, they will lend themselves to the destructive side. The story of these three siblings is quite interesting, especially when we consider the fact that Moses grew up most of his life not knowing he was related to Miriam and Aaron.

> "Sibling rivalry is the jealousy, competition and fighting between brothers and sisters. It is a concern for almost all parents of two or more kids. Problems often start right after the birth of the second child. Sibling rivalry usually continues throughout childhood and can be very frustrating and stressful to parents.
> Fortunately, there are lots of things parents can do to help their kids get along better and work through conflicts in positive ways.
> Further, most likely your kids' relationship will eventually develop into a close one. Working things out with siblings gives your children a chance to develop important skills like cooperating and being able to see another person's point of view."
> Source: C.S. Mott Children's Hospital Michigan Medicine

The circumstances under which he is introduced to them could have only been orchestrated by God. Knowing Moses' story, we know his upbringing and the upbringing of his siblings had been totally different. The amazing thing is when God is ready to use you, He will pull you from wherever He finds you.

God's plan for Moses started long before he was born. However, Moses had to go through this process to be able to accomplish the assignment on his life. We do not always understand God's ways, but we know they always work together for our good. Moses' story should give every believer hope. It does not matter where you currently find yourself, when God is ready to call you forth, He will find you, even if you are on the back side of the desert. Let us see what caused Miriam and Aaron to question Moses' authority.

Numbers 12:1-15 states, "Miriam and Aaron began to talk against Moses because of his Cushite wife, for he had married a Cushite. 'Has the LORD spoken only through Moses?' they asked. 'Hasn't he also spoken through us?' And the LORD heard this. (Now Moses was a very humble man, more humble than anyone else on the face of the Earth.) At once the LORD said to Moses, Aaron and Miriam, 'Come out to the tent of meeting, all three of you.' So, the three of them went out. Then the LORD came down in a pillar of cloud; he stood at the entrance to the tent and summoned Aaron and Miriam. When the two of them stepped forward, he said, "Listen to my words:'
'When there is a prophet among you, I, the LORD, reveal myself to them in visions, I speak to them in dreams. But this is not true of my servant Moses; he is faithful in all my house." With him I speak face to face, clearly and not in riddles; he sees the form of the LORD.

Why then were you not afraid to speak against my servant Moses?' The anger of the LORD burned against them, and he left them. When the cloud lifted from above the tent, Miriam's skin was leprous—it became as white as snow. Aaron turned toward her and saw that she had a defiling skin disease, and he said to Moses, 'Please, my lord, I ask you not to hold against us the sin we have so foolishly committed. Do not let her be like a stillborn infant coming from its mother's womb with its flesh half eaten away.' So Moses cried out to the LORD, 'Please, God, heal her!' The LORD replied to Moses, 'If her father had spit in her face, would she not have been in disgrace for seven days? Confine her outside the camp for seven days; after that she can be brought back.' So Miriam was confined outside the camp for seven days, and the people did not move on till she was brought back."

Both Miriam and Aaron questioned Moses' authority; why Miriam was the only one punished puzzles me. It appeared that Aaron was just as guilty as Miriam, however, God laid the responsibility on Miriam. Could it have been because of the difference in their hearts' postures? According to scripture, Miriam was the one who initiated the conversation, therefore, she was the one who had to suffer the consequences.

In the body of Christ, we can be guilty at times of challenging the authority of those God has placed over us. However, we must keep in mind that we do not get to decide who should or should not lead. Our place is to trust God's authority and leave the rest to Him. Leadership has the weighted responsibility of leading God's people. If their motives or actions are not pure, they will have God to answer to and suffer the consequences as well. Just keep in mind, the measure you mete will be measured to you.

Those that lead God's people should remember they are only under-shepherds; Jesus is the true Shepherd. The Word of God teaches us the Good Shepherd gives His life for the sheep. The Good Shepherd leaves the ninety-nine and goes after the one. I believe everyone who has any type of leadership role in the body of Christ should study the ultimate leader, Jesus Christ. Jesus led the twelve apostles. What could be more challenging than having three years to prepare and train twelve men (less one) to facilitate discipleship in the Earth?

We very seldom see Jesus' leadership style today; we didn't see Jesus lording His authority and position over His disciples. Jesus understood that it would take time to groom those that were called to walk alongside Him. He exhibited great patience for the disciples. He was available to answer their questions and to encourage them in their shortcomings. He could see past their current states and see who they were becoming.

Jesus paid a price that no one else could have paid for His Church. I admonish every leader to consider the length God went through to make sure His children had a way back to Him. The scripture cautions us to be careful how we build upon the foundation that Jesus built. The Word of God teaches us that those who are teachers will be held to a higher standard. God expects those who represent Him to His people to not misrepresent His heart towards them.

1 Corinthians 3:10-11 KJV reads, "According to the grace of God, which is given unto me, as a wise master-builder, I have laid the foundation, and another buildeth thereon. But let every man take heed how he buildeth thereupon. For other foundation can no man lay than that is laid, which is Jesus Christ."

We understand that God called Moses to lead the people; Aaron and Miriam were called to assist him. It wasn't Miriam's place to correct Moses. In correcting Moses, she was, in turn, attempting to correct God. Why Aaron went along with her plan was probably because she was the oldest of the three of them. God knew who Moses was married to when He calledhim. God also knew the sacrifice Moses would have to make in order to accomplish the assignment God had placed on his life.

Miriam didn't understand that she didn't have the authority to dictate to Moses how God was leading him, nor could she arbitrarily step in and take command of what God spoke to him concerning God's plan for leading His people. Basically, what Miriam was saying is—God, You chose the wrong person to carry out this assignment, so I'm going to step in and make sure everything is carried out just the way You intended for them to go. Imagine Miriam correcting God and convincing her brother, Aaron, to go along with her in her rebellion.

God does not always give us the full picture of what He has placed in the minds and hearts of the ones He has called to lead us. However, when He calls a man or woman to a specific assignment in the Kingdom of God, He expects us to follow them as if we are following Him. But He does not expect us to follow them without them first following Him. Jesus had to rebuke Peter for trying to interfere with the purpose for which He was sent into the world. We should support those in leadership, for every great and effectual door that is opened unto them, there is an adversary waiting on the other side. Let us be the ones that take the adversary out.

There are those who covet the role of leadership in the church for pure reasons and some for impure reasons. Just bear in mind that many are called, but few are chosen. I believe few are chosen because there is a level of concentration and purity that God requires out of those who wield His sword. You will be tried in the fire, and only that which remains will stand. That's when you realize that your life is not your own; you've been brought with a price.

> "It could have been one of the worst leadership experiences Moses had. For days and days, he watched and participated, somehow, in God's word making. He was with the Almighty as he wrote the clear set of ten rules for the people of God. Surrounding him was decadently terrifying power which seems to have been climbing up and down the mountain. And Moses was at its peak.

Then, commandments in hand, he walked – or perhaps in his excitement ran – down the mountain to his people. There are probably hundreds of paintings on the subject. It's always Aaron standing above the people eliciting worship for a shiny baby cow. Aaron was both submitting to the people's desire to worship something other than the Terrifying and inciting them, or leading them, to it. It's some sort of otherworldly dance of god party. And Aaron, Moses' big brother, was at its heart (interestingly, Miriam was not present in this story).

Moses was angry. God? Well, the community of Israel drank their own sin and death crippled them.

Aaron had stood leading it all. He'd listened well to the people. He'd helped them find a something to worship. He'd set up that old golden statue and an altar for it. He'd let them run wild with worship toward something other than El Shaddai. He'd set up a meal of fellowship and sacrifice for it. And the sounds of war-song throbbed from the community— this was how wild, the worship was. Aaron led it all.

But, perhaps, both God and Moses saw something different that day. Though Aaron was completely wrong and was working under shadow instead of light, perhaps God saw in Aaron a destiny. Perhaps he knew what destiny he'd make from this shadowed leadership. Certainly, the entire community of Israel had felt comfortable talking with Aaron about their issues, their fears of the loss of God himself. He knew how to hear them with compassion. He knew how to lead them into and for worship. He knew how to organize worshipful celebration.

Instead of just seeing leadership toward evil, God saw and used the raw leadership that had been gifted to Moses' brother. He did not demote Aaron but redirected Aaron's talents for his own glory. Aaron became the first high priest of God and Israel: chosen and set apart by the Almighty himself. He became the first example of priestly holiness—being set apart for and with and by God. Aaron used his skills to draw Israel into warrior shouts for their Redeemer, for the implementation of celebration, for sacrifice on the altar of God. Instead of seeing only failure, God saw future and made something out of it. God took the shadowy leadership of Aaron into Light."

Source: Leading from the Shadow by Jessica Fleck

Moses was very compassionate towards his brother and sister. When Aaron asked him to petition God on Miriam's behalf, he did not hesitate to do so. He could have allowed bitterness to get the best of him, but he knew he would need them to accomplish his assignment. We know Miriam was restored and went on to do great exploits for God. I believe if asked the question, "Am I my brother's keeper?" Miriam, Aaron, and Moses' answer would be a resounding yes.

Joshua and Caleb

But the whole community began to talk about stoning Joshua and Caleb. Then the glorious presence of the LORD appeared to all the Israelites at the Tabernacle.
Numbers 14:10 (NLT)

The story of Joshua and Caleb is a familiar one. They are remembered as the only two of the twelve spies that Moses sent to spy out the land who'd returned with a good report. At this place and time, the Israelites had little fight left in them. When faced with hardships, their first inclination was to go back to Egypt. After spending four hundred years in slavery, it is understandable why the Israelites would see themselves as grasshoppers in their own sight. However, at the hands of Moses, they'd seen miracles and watched God perform His Word. In all honesty, getting past a slavery mindset is not as easy as we may think. The story of Joshua and Caleb is one of faith versus fear, but the question we must ask ourselves is—how bad did they want it?

When God sent Moses to Pharaoh demanding him to let His people go, the motivation behind the request was so that God's people could go and worship Him. The reason for their leaving Egypt seemed to have gotten lost somewhere along the way. There appeared to have been more complaining than worshiping. The Israelites were promised a land flowing with milk and honey. You would think that after spending four hundred years in Egypt as slaves, the thought of their own land would have been motivation enough. I believe most of them likely heard oral traditions of how after being in slavery, God would deliver them from their enemies. The idea that they would have to fight for it was more than some of the Israelites were able to comprehend.

Let us look a little deeper into what their mindsets may have been during this time. For four hundred years, their every move was dictated by someone else. There was no freedom of expression or thought without the end results being death. The idea of freedom must have been as foreign as the land they now found themselves in. All of a sudden, they had to think for themselves, and they were not sure what life really looked like outside of Egypt. At least in Egypt, from sun-up to sun-down, their days were based on a routine and they knew when and what they would eat. After years of praying for deliverance, somehow obtaining it was a bit more than they could handle. Unfortunately, we do not always make the best decisions, and in this case, neither did the Israelites.

We must admit there were circumstances and situations in our lives that seemed like Egypt to us. These were the places of bondage that, no matter how hard we tried, we could not overcome them on our own. The world's system had such a pull and hold on our mindsets that the very thought of giving up our old ways to do things God's way was all-out war. If we are honest, for a lot of us, it took some time for us to leave the land of carnality and fully embrace the land of maturity. The battle begins in the mind; we war against old mindsets and our own ways of doing life. The only way we can win this battle is through Jesus Christ. The Word of God teaches us that Christ in us is our only hope of glory.

Like the Israelites, God called us out of the world to worship Him. We cannot lose sight of how important this is to God. Let us define worship. "Worship is an act of religious devotion usually directed towards a deity. For many, worship is not about an emotion, it is more about a recognition of God. An act of worship may be performed individually, in an informal or formal group, or by a designated leader. Such acts may involve honoring" (Source: Wikipedia). God must be exalted above all else; this includes all circumstances, situations, and whatever life throws our way. In hindsight, we can see how the Israelites allowed fear to keep them in the wilderness much longer than God intended for them to be there. Now that we have the understanding, how will we move on to what God has called us to?

What are some of the promises of God that were spoken over your life that have yet to manifest in the natural realm? Please be mindful that we have to war for the promises of God. There are times when God proves us through our difficulties, and how we handle those difficulties determines the speed at which our promises are fulfilled. Complaining is not the objective when it comes to having faith in what God has spoken over your life. Now, back to the Israelites. The Israelites postponed their entry into the promised land by allowing fear to paralyze them in an old season. It was never God's intention for the Israelites to spend forty years in the wilderness, His plan was to give them houses they did not build and land they did not purchase.

Moses had the difficult task of leading God's people out of Egypt and into the promised land as God instructed him. We know from the Bible that Moses became frustrated with the children of Israel, and his frustration led him to misrepresent God. Were the children of Israel difficult? Absolutely, but even in their difficulties, God had a plan for them. How do you lead people out of four hundred years of slavery and keep your sanity? We know Moses was challenged by the children of Israel, but he was God's choice, so everything he needed to accomplish the task had been provided by God. However, Moses' challenges did not excuse him from leading the children of Israel to the promised land. The complaining and rebellion of the children of Israel did not sit well with God. Their complaining delayed their entry into promised land by forty years.

When it comes to Caleb, the Bible referred to him as having a different spirit. What does that mean? Caleb took God at His Word. He was not relying on his own strength; the promise came from God so he expected God to fulfill it. By the time the Israelites finally made it to the promised land and the twelve tribes were assigned their specific areas, Caleb was eighty-years old. At eighty years old, you would think Caleb was ready to settle down and rest, but not Caleb. This is when Caleb asked Joshua for his mountain.

"Now therefore give me this mountain, whereof the LORD spake in that day; for thou heardest in that day how the Anakims were there, and that the cities were great and fenced: if so, be the LORD will be with me, then I shall be able to drive them out, as the LORD said. And Joshua blessed him and gave unto Caleb the son of Jephunneh Hebron for an inheritance. Hebron therefore became the inheritance of Caleb the son of Jephunneh the Kenezite unto this day, because that he wholly followed the LORD God of Israel (Joshua 14:12-14).

Let me point out something here. I noticed when it came to Joshua, he did not initially speak up with Caleb when it came to taking the land. Numbers13:30 reads, "And Caleb stilled the people before Moses, and said, let us go up at once, and possess it; for we are well able to overcome it." It was not until Numbers14:6 that we saw Joshua agreeing with Caleb. "And Joshua the son of Nun, and Caleb the son of Jephunneh, *which were* of them that searched the land, rent their clothes." Why Joshua did not immediately speak up with Caleb puzzles me, but I am sure there is a simple explanation. More than likely, Caleb spoke up first so there was no need for Joshua to speak at that time.

"If you look into the meaning of Caleb, you probably come up with an answer "dog." According to most dictionaries, the name Caleb means "dog." At first glance, Caleb's name may sound too derogatory and insulting. Who would name his son with a name that means dog, right? But here we are. We encounter a mighty warrior, a man of valor, a man who fully followed God and his name means dog.

However, there is a *significance* to the meaning of Caleb's name. First of all, he possesses the FAITHFULNESS of a dog. There's no doubt, we know today that a dog is man's best friend because of their great LOYALTY to their master. You might have heard of a story of a dog's love to his master. In the same way, we must also emulate this attribute of a dog. Our loyalty and allegiance are for God alone.

Moreover, a dog is there to protect his master. I have also seen dogs who are willing to give their lives just to save their master. And that is exactly what we must learn from dogs.

While yes, having a name that means "a dog" can be very disappointing especially in the Israelite society where names are considered to be a determiner of their fate, Caleb didn't see it that way. Instead, he made it a point that he will demonstrate the positive attributes of dogs in his life."

Source: The Meaning Behind the Name Caleb by joshuainfantado

"Joshua the Faithful Warrior and Leader. Moses gave Joshua his name, meaning, "the Lord has delivered." The change from his former name, Hoshea ("he has delivered, " Num. 13:16 ; Deut. 32:44), reflects a confession of the God of Israel as Savior. Joshua first appears in Israel's war with the Amalekites (Exodus 17:8-13). He fights on behalf of Moses and leads Israel to victory. He thus personifies Israel at war. When he reappears in Exodus 24:13, Joshua climbs Mount Sinai alongside Moses. Later (32:17), Joshua warns Moses of the noise that comes from the camp below where Israel engages in idolatry. He joins Moses in the covenant-making process and in watching over its preservation. With Caleb, Joshua spies out the land and returns a positive evaluation of the possibilities of Israelite occupation (Num. 14). He appreciates and bears witness to the promised land as God's gift to Israel. Finally, Joshua is designated as Moses' successor and is commissioned to succeed him."

Source: Joshua, Theology of by Richard S. Hess

The lesson for us in this is—we should never give up on our promises. It does not matter how long it may take or how old we may be. If we persevere, we will obtain the promise. We know from the Word of God that Joshua took Moses' place in leading the children of Israel after Moses' death. Joshua was faithful in his service to Moses and his obedience to God. I believe if we follow the principles behind the story of Joshua and Caleb, we will understand that when we work together regarding the instructions and the plans given to us by God, we will come together as one and see the power of God; this is when we keep our faith in God and not in ourselves.

Our question remains the same. Am I my brother's keeper? The answer continues to be yes.

Hophni and Phinehas

When we first meet Eli, he is sitting by the doorpost of the tabernacle, watching Hannah as she makes her vow to the Lord and prays for a son. Eli automatically assumes that Hannah is drunk because he sees her lips moving but no words are coming out of her mouth. This speaks to Eli's discernment or lack thereof, but given the fact that Hannah and her husband had just finished eating and drinking, I guess it was reasonable for Eli to assume she may have indulged in too much wine. However, Eli did bless Hannah and he sent her on her way.

My heart goes out to Eli. After spending forty years judging Israel as High Priest, Eli didn't realize by praying for Hannah to get pregnant with a son, his priesthood was about to change. The moment he prayed for Hannah to give birth, his replacement was already in the womb. I don't want to make light of the responsibilities that Eli carried as High Priest. The fact that he served for forty years lets us know that he himself walked before God with a certain level of reverential fear. We know that whenever the High Priest was about to go into the Holy of Holies to offer sacrifices on behalf of the people, a rope was tied around his waist to drag him out if he himself wasn't pure. So, whenever the High Priest would go into the Holy of Holies, he didn't know if he would make it out. One can only imagine the fear and stress he had to be under not knowing if his cleansing ceremony would be acceptable to

God. But year after year, he had to do the same ritual on behalf of himself and on behalf of the people of Israel.

From scripture, we know that Hannah gave birth to a son and called him Samuel, meaning "God has heard" or "name of God." Hannah kept her promise that she would lend the child back to God. When the child was weaned from his mother, she took him to the house of the Lord to live with Eli. When you consider how Eli raised Samuel, the question that comes to mind is—why didn't he train his own sons the same way he raised Samuel? The scripture doesn't say whether Eli's wife played a role in raising Samuel, since he was such a young child when his mother brought him to the house of God. In hindsight, maybe he was intentional in not allowing Samuel to become like his sons, but somewhere along the way, his sons didn't get the proper training needed to minister in the house of the Lord. Unfortunately, this can be seen all too often in the house of the Lord. We have those who see the house of God as an opportunity to advance themselves, rather than as an opportunity to represent God.

What does that look like for us today? For those of us who serve the man or woman of God, it's important that we serve them in such a way that we represent them well before the people of God. We shouldn't allow the brokenness in us to cause the people of God to have a disdain for the things of God. Let us be mindful to keep our bodies under subjection so that after we have ministered to others, we ourselves will not be cast away. The Word of God says, "And if ye have not been faithful in that which is another man's, who shall give you that which is your own?" (Luke 16:12).

"Now the sons of Eli were wicked men; they had no regard for the LORD or for the custom of the priests with the people."
1 Samuel 2:12-13 (BSB)

Eli and his sons are examples of what happens when fathers refuse to discipline their sons. As God's Priest, Eli had the responsibility to represent God to the people and the people to God. Since Eli was Priest, his sons were also priests. However, they lacked the reverential fear of God required to execute their office, and they treated what was offered to God with contempt. The dictionary's definition of a priest is "one especially consecrated to the service of a divinity and through whom worship, prayer, sacrifice, or other service is offered to the object of worship - and pardon, blessing, or deliverance is obtained by the worshipper" (Source: Funk and Wagnall Vol. 21 p.273)

What does that look like for us today? For those whom God has placed over His house and over His people, it is important that we represent God well before the people. The offering is sacred to God; we are reminded of this when Jesus stood over the offering to see what the people were giving.

Mark 12:41-44 reads, "Now Jesus sat opposite the treasury and saw how the people put money into the treasury. And many *who were* rich put in much. Then one poor widow came and threw in two mites, which make a quadrans. So He called His disciples to *Himself* and said to them, 'Assuredly, I say to you that this poor widow has put in more than all those who have given to the treasury; for they all put in out of their abundance, but she out of her poverty put in all that she had, her whole livelihood.'"

Luke 21:1-4 says, "And He looked up and saw the rich putting their gifts into the treasury, and He saw also a certain poor widow putting in two mites. So He said, 'Truly I say to you that this poor widow has put in more than all; for all these out of their abundance have put in offerings for God, but she out of her poverty put in all the livelihood that she had.'"

The offerings of God's people represent their sweat and labor and should be treated as such. The offerings should assist those who are over the house of God in serving the people and the house of God. It is not for those who represent Him to misuse and lavish the offerings upon themselves. At the same time, God expects His people to bring their offerings before Him reverentially and willingly, for there is a blessing associated with the offering.

Eli should have taken the complaints against his sons more seriously. If possible, he should have removed them from their posts and dealt with them concerning their misconduct. He allowed the people of God to suffer under the hands of his sons, and they dishonored God in the process. 1 Sam. 2:17 says, "Thus the sin of these young men was severe in the sight of the LORD, for they were treating the LORD's offering with contempt."

1 Samuel 22-25 reads, "Now Eli was very old, and he heard about everything his sons were doing to all Israel and how they were sleeping with the women who served at the entrance to the Tent of Meeting. 'Why are you doing these things?' Eli said to his sons. 'I hear about your wicked deeds from all these people. No, my sons; it is not a good report I hear circulating among the LORD's people. If a man sins against another man, God can intercede for him; but if a man sins against the LORD, who can intercede for him?' But they would not listen to their father, since the LORD intended to put them to death."

1 Samuel 31-34 goes on to say, "Behold, the days are coming when I will cut off your strength and the strength of your father's house, so that no older man will be left in your house. You will see distress in My dwelling place. Despite all that is good in Israel, no one in your house will ever again reach old age. And every one of you that I do not cut off from My altar, your eyes will fail, and your heart will grieve. All your descendants will die by the sword of men. And this sign shall come to you concerning your two sons Hophni and Phinehas: They will both die on the same day."

One can make the argument that Eli tried to discipline his sons, but they would not listen. It was up to Eli as Priest to make sure that the house of God remained holy and was honored in the sight of the people. As the people of God, we should never allow God to be despised in the eyes of

69

His people based on our actions. In his old age, Eli was losing sight of the importance of his obligation to the house of God.

Since we understand there is kindness and severity to God, we should not presuppose that God will overlook our disobedience. Even in this age of grace, it should be the love of Christ that constrains us. We are under a better covenant than Eli and his sons were. Jesus' sacrifice for us should outweigh any sin or challenge we are faced with. We can do all things through Christ who strengthens us.

Unfortunately for Eli and his sons, they did not repent and turn from their wicked ways. The sons of Eli placed their flesh above God, and Eli placed his sons above God. The Word of God was given to Eli and the fulfillment was on the way. We must be quick to repent and turn from anything that would cause us to dishonor God.

Eli was warned by Samuel about what would happen because he did not discipline his sons. In his old age, Eli must have grown weary in the process of carrying out his duties to God's people. I am sure his sons frustrated him with their disobedience and lack of reverence for the things of God. Because of their disobedience, God vowed that the family of Eli would not be forgiven.

It's a sad commentary on Eli to have served Israel for forty years and his sons did not know God. What's worse is Eli's sons had no respect for their father. Even if they didn't know God, they should have respected Eli enough to not blatantly sin before the people of Israel. One can only wonder what the interactions between Samuel and the sons of Eli must have been like. It was obvious that Eli had very little control over his sons and their actions, so much so that God prophesied through Samuel that the whole lineage of Eli would be removed from the face of the Earth by God Himself. There's no indication that Eli made any changes after receiving the prophetic word from Samuel. He didn't fall on his face and repent before God, nor did he cry out for mercy. Eli's only response was, "It is the Lord. Let Him do what seems good to Him." We know why the Word of the Lord was rare in those days; it was because Eli honored his sons more than he honored the house of the Lord. Eli had lost his vision for the things of God, and it was only a matter time before he allowed the ark of the covenant of God to be taken by the Philistines.

It would be years before the ark of the covenant made it back into the hands of God's covenant people. The Philistines placed the ark of the covenant among their gods, making God common among their gods. There was no reverential fear for God among the Philistines, but we know from scripture that this was short-lived.

Let us take note of how Eli became weary in his ministry unto the Lord and to God's people. When we refuse to honor God and His house, God will remove us from our positions and replace us with those who will be obedient to Him. Let us repent for not putting God first and for not giving Him priority in every area of our lives. It's time to put God back on the throne of His house, the nations of the world, the family unit and the seven mountains in the Earth.

"There are several lessons to be learned from the experiences of Eli and his sons. As a priest of the Lord, Eli successfully supervised Samuel at the tabernacle but was not as diligent as he could have been toward his own sons. In a similar fashion, although many endeavors may be worthy of our time and attention, we ought not to neglect our responsibility toward our family because of our devotion to other activities. The First Presidency recently stated, "We counsel parents and children to give the highest priority to family prayer, family home evening, gospel study and instruction, and wholesome family activities. However worthy and appropriate other demands or activities may be, they must not be permitted to displace the divinely-appointed duties that only parents and families can adequately perform." As President David O. McKay taught, "No other success can compensate for failure in the home." We must learn by the Spirit how to strike the proper balance between family and other responsibilities.

Further, we should not assume that parents are culpable for the poor conduct of their children. Many righteous parents earnestly strive to teach their children from their youth the principles of the gospel, yet their children still go astray. At the same time, however, we must not downplay the crucial responsibility of parents to instruct their children.

President Gordon B. Hinckley has given the following counsel:

I recognize that there are parents who, notwithstanding an outpouring of love and a diligent and faithful effort to teach them, see their children grow in a contrary manner and weep while their wayward sons and daughters willfully pursue courses of tragic consequence. For such I have great sympathy, and to them I am wont to quote the words of Ezekiel: "The son shall not bear the iniquity of the father, neither shall the father bear the iniquity of the son" (Ezekiel 18:20).

But such is the exception rather than the rule. Nor does the exception justify others of us from making every effort in showing forth love, example, and correct precept in the rearing of those for whom God has given us sacred responsibility."

Finally, we understand that the family unit is at the heart of the gospel of Jesus Christ. In the inspired declaration "The Family: A Proclamation to the World," the First Presidency and the Quorum of the Twelve Apostles solemnly affirmed, "Parents have a sacred duty to rear their children in love and righteousness, to provide for their physical and spiritual needs, to teach them to love and serve one another, to observe the commandments of God and to be law-abiding citizens wherever they live. Husbands and wives—mothers and fathers—will be held accountable before God for the discharge of these obligations."

The story of Eli and his sons reminds us of the serious responsibility parents have to teach their children the principles of the gospel of Jesus Christ and the heartbreaking consequences that can result if parents neglect this sacred obligation."
Source: Eli and His Sons Frank F. Judd Jr.

I can't emphasize enough how important the role of the father is in the family unit. We understand that the man, from God's perspective, is considered the priest of the home, however, if that man doesn't have a relationship with God, it would be impossible for him to represent God to his family. What happens when the father is in the home but missing in the family? This is what we see in the life of Eli and his family. Somewhere along the way, Eli didn't instill in his sons the reverential fear of the Lord, and as a result, he lost control of his sons.

It's a dangerous thing for a priest to make the presence of the Lord a common thing among his family. How much better would our families be if the priest of the home took his position seriously? The Word of God teaches us that those who are born again are kings and priests to our God. Positionally, God allows us the opportunity to minister to the people on His behalf, but we also get to represent the royalty of God in the Earth.

We don't have the luxury of becoming weary when it comes to the things of God. What we have to do is differentiate between what's us and what's God. If Jesus' yoke is easy and His burden is light, maybe we should check what we are yoked to and whose burden we are carrying. When we are moving in God's strength, there should be a measure of joy in our pursuits.

Eli should have passed his priesthood on to his sons. Instead, his legacy ended with his death and the death of his sons. Worst still, he allowed the ark of the covenant to be taken captive by the Philistines. As a budding prophet, Samuel had the hard task of giving the word of correction from the Lord to the one who should have given the Word of the Lord to him.

"Am I my brother's keeper?" Yes, Lord!

TAMAR AND AMNON

The story of Tamar is one of justice and injustice, one where being the daughter of the king doesn't exempt you from injustice's horrendous effects. However, when the injustice is an inside job perpetrated from within the king's domain by someone you are related to, where do you turn? I'm sure, however, that nowadays, after a few sessions of therapy and counseling, everything would be just fine. Unfortunately for Tamar, no amount of therapy or counseling would change her sentence.

Incest among families wasn't anything new in their time, just like it's not new in our time. In fact, during their time, inter-familial marriage was common among royal families. The problem in our time that many would like to brush under the rug is the damage that is done to an entire generation. Regrettably, there are many men and women who are bound today because they were told to get over it and move on with their lives after having been inappropriately touched by one or more members of their families. I believe mental illnesses come in many forms. There must be a level of mental instability that hunts those who try to make sense of why those who should have provided protection for them, instead brought them harm.

Regarding the perpetrators, it is a common saying that often what is done to us, we do to others. This may be true to an extent, but should it continue to be the norm?

Can you imagine the number of people who walk through life keeping their secrets and praying that no one will ever find out, because they blame themselves for the shortcomings of others? To my brothers and sisters who have suffered at the hands of those who should have protected you, please don't continue to hide behind your pain. Jesus died for you, and grace is available for your healing.

The Word of God teaches that Satan comes to steal, kill and to destroy, but Jesus came that we may have life and life more abundantly. Satan doesn't care who or what he uses to separate us from God if he can keep us blaming God for everything that ever went wrong in our lives. I'm sure anyone who has cried out to God for help in the middle of their struggle and didn't receive it, had that moment when they felt as if God just didn't care about what they were going through.

Let's think about Tamar and her situation. As a member of the royal family, there was no reason for her to believe that her life would be different than any other woman of royalty in the king's house. One act of uncontrollable temptation from her own brother would change that forever. I'm sure Tamar seemed to be out of his reach. Amnon thought his love for Tamar was genuine and heartfelt, however, once his lust was satisfied, he realized it was only fleeting, at best. Unlike Tamar, Amnon was secure in his role as a son of the king. He didn't think twice about sending Tamar away. It was almost as if he knew there would be no consequences for his actions.

Who do you turn to when the hardships of life cause irreversible heartache and there's nothing anyone can say or do to change it? For example, when a couple experiences the loss of a child because of a miscarriage after trying for years, is there anything anyone can say or do that can bring comfort to them in that moment? Even for the believers in Christ, these are the moments that try men's souls.

As we read the story of Tamar and Amnon, it's easy to point the finger at Amnon and his wickedness, but what about us? As members of the body of Christ, we have an obligation to our brothers and sisters as well. If we are honest, whether intentionally or unintentionally, we have injured a brother or a sister and walked away leaving them wounded. There comes a time in our walk with God when we must take responsibility for our own actions and not be a conduit for the enemy to take our brothers and sisters out.

To my brothers in Christ, please know that the women of God are not there for target practice until you find your wife. Keep in mind that they will be someone else's wife one day, so the same level of respect and honor you want for your wife, please give it to your sisters in Christ. To my sisters in Christ, it's not just up to the brothers to respect and honor you. You must come to a place in your life where you respect and honor your own self. Stop allowing the world's system to dictate how you do relationships. We should all acknowledge God in all our ways and allow Him to direct our paths. Acknowledging God doesn't mean you don't have a choice in the matter, it just means you should be making better choices.

I would like to suggest that, at some point in your walk with Christ, His love for you should constrain you. Because of the sacrifice Jesus made on your behalf, you should be willing to make sacrifices on the behalf of others. What does that look like? It looks like when an opportunity presents itself to keep someone from making a mistake that can affect them for the rest of their lives, instead of choosing to satisfy your flesh, choose to walk in integrity. This goes both ways. Women don't lay with someone who is not married to you, and men don't allow yourself to be used as past-time fun just to satisfy an urge.

Trust me, there are consequences to them both. How many marriages have been ruined because of an impulse or lack of restraint, and how many children were born out of loneliness and boredom? Let's not continue the same cycles of dysfunction and wonder why our marriages and families don't work. We are no longer in the world and our lives should reflect our newness in Christ.

I understand we come to Christ with a lot of our issues intact, but it's time we change the trajectory of our bloodlines by learning what's missing in our lives, and then allowing Christ to be for us what we couldn't be for ourselves. There's nothing wrong with admitting you have a lack of understanding in an area, but be open to God sending men and women to help you get the understanding you need. Let's stop allowing the enemy to use us to inflict pain on one another. Before you act, consider the long-term consequences of your actions and ask yourself—is there something I can do to help my brother or sister? Then reflect on what would Jesus do.

"In the course of time, Amnon son of David fell in love with Tamar, the beautiful sister of Absalom son of David."
2 Samuel 13:1 (NIV)

The story of Tamar and Amnon is one of the more difficult topics to deal with. Unfortunately, some in the church are guilty of perpetrating this sin against sisters and brothers in the body of Christ. Let me be very clear here, God has reserved sex for marriage. Sex outside of marriage is sin regardless of whether it is consensual or non-consensual. Many of us have engaged in sexual activity prior to coming to Christ and some after coming to Christ. We know that "If we confess our sins, he is faithful and just to forgive us our sins, and to cleanse us from all unrighteousness" (1John 1:9).

There comes a time, nonetheless, when we must, "lay aside every weight, and the sin which doth so easily beset us, and let us run with patience the race that is set before us" (Hebrews 12:1). When we come to Christ, we no longer have to trust in our own strength to keep us from sinning. God has given us the Holy Spirit to lead and guide us into all truth. The truth of the matter is, we make the sacrifice of Jesus ineffective in our lives when we continue to willfully sin. God has made provision for sin, but it should no longer be a lifestyle.

Given the fact that Tamar and Amnon are siblings, Amnon ought to have protected Tamar at all costs.

2 Samuel 13:1-19 tells the story. It reads, "In the course of time, Amnon, son of David fell in love with Tamar, the beautiful sister of Absalom son of David. Amnon became so obsessed with his sister Tamar that he made himself ill. She was a virgin, and it seemed impossible for him to do anything to her. Now Amnon had an adviser named Jonadab son of Shimeah, David's brother. Jonadab was a very shrewd man. He asked Amnon, 'Why do you, the king's son, look so haggard morning after morning? Won't you tell me?' Amnon said to him, 'I'm in love with Tamar, my brother Absalom's sister.' 'Go to bed and pretend to be ill,' Jonadab said. 'When your father comes to see you, say to him, 'I would like my sister Tamar to come and give me something to eat. Let her prepare the food in my sight so I may watch her and then eat it from her hand.' So Amnon lay down and pretended to be ill. When the king came to see him, Amnon said to him, 'I would like my sister Tamar to come and make some special bread in my sight, so I may eat from her hand.' David sent word to Tamar at the palace: 'Go to the house of your brother Amnon and prepare some food for him.' So Tamar went to the house of her brother Amnon, who was lying down. She took some dough, kneaded it, made the bread in his sight, and baked it. Then she took the pan and served him the bread, but he refused to eat. 'Send everyone out of here,' Amnon said. So, everyone left him. Then Amnon said to Tamar, 'Bring the food here into my bedroom so I may eat from your hand.' And Tamar took the bread she had prepared and

brought it to her brother Amnon in his bedroom. But when she took it to him to eat, he grabbed her and said, 'Come to bed with me, my sister.'

'No, my brother!' she said to him. 'Don't force me! Such a thing should not be done in Israel! Don't do this wicked thing. What about me? Where could I get rid of my disgrace? And what about you? You would be like one of the wicked fools in Israel. Please speak to the king; he will not keep me from being married to you.' But he refused to listen to her, and since he was stronger than she, he raped her. Then Amnon hated her with intense hatred. In fact, he hated her more than he had loved her. Amnon said to her, 'Get up and get out!'

'No!' she said to him. 'Sending me away would be a greater wrong than what you have already done to me.'

But he refused to listen to her. He called his personal servant and said, 'Get this woman out of my sight and bolt the door after her.' So his servant put her out and bolted the door after her. She was wearing an ornate robe, for this was the kind of garment the virgin daughters of the king wore. Tamar put ashes on her head and tore the ornate robe she was wearing. She put her hands on her head and went away, weeping aloud as she went."

There are so many issues we can address here. Pondering the fact that Tamar was the virgin daughter of King David and Amnon was her brother, why would Jonadab, who was Tamar's cousin, devise such a wicked scheme against her? Tamar knew that, as a virgin daughter of the king, to be sexually defiled meant she could never marry. Amnon also understood that if he did not marry Tamar, she could never marry, which makes what he did to her even more wicked. As she walked away from Amnon's house, every step she took was a reminder of how her status as a single woman would never change.

Surely, her father, King David would come to her rescue. Perhaps, he would force Amnon to marry her. King David's response to his daughter's defilement, however, is a little disappointing, so we see her brother Absalom come to her aid.

2 Samuel 13:20-39 reads, "And Absalom her brother said unto her, Hath Amnon thy brother been with thee? But hold now thy peace, my sister: he is thy brother; regard not this thing. So, Tamar remained desolate in her brother Absalom's house. But when king David heard of all these things, he was very wroth. And Absalom spake unto his brother Amnon neither good nor bad: for Absalom hated Amnon, because he had forced his sister Tamar. And it came to pass after two full years, that Absalom had sheepshearers in Baalhazor, which is beside Ephraim: and Absalom invited all the king's sons. And Absalom came to the king, and said, Behold, now, thy servant hath sheepshearers; let the king, I beseech thee, and his servants go with thy servant. And the king said to Absalom, Nay, my son, let us not all now go, lest we be chargeable unto thee. And he pressed him: howbeit he would not go but blessed him. Then said Absalom, If, not I pray thee, let my brother Amnon go with us. And the king said unto him, Why, should he go with thee? But Absalom pressed him, that he let Amnon, and all the king's sons go

with him. Now Absalom had commanded his servants, saying, Mark ye now when Amnon's heart is merry with wine, and when I say unto you, Smite Amnon; then kill him, fear not: have not I commanded you? be courageous, and be valiant. And the servants of Absalom did unto Amnon as Absalom had commanded. Then all the king's sons arose, and every man gat him up upon his mule, and fled. And it came to pass, while they were in the way, that tidings came to David, saying, Absalom hath slain all the king's sons, and there is not one of them left. Then the king arose, and tare his garments, and lay on the Earth; and all his servants stood by with their clothes rent. And Jonadab, the son of Shimeah David's brother, answered and said, Let, not my lord suppose that they have slain all the young men the king's sons; for Amnon only is dead: for by the appointment of Absalom this hath been determined from the day that he forced his sister Tamar. Now therefore let not my lord the king take the thing to his heart, to think that all the king's sons are dead: for Amnon only is dead. But Absalom fled. And the young man that kept the watch lifted, up his eyes, and looked, and behold, there came much, people by the way of the hill side behind him. And Jonadab said unto the king, Behold, the king's sons come: as thy servant said, so it is. And it came to pass, as soon as he had made an end of speaking, that, behold, the king's sons came, and lifted, up their voice and wept: and the king also and all his servants wept very sore. But Absalom fled, and went to Talmai, the son of Ammihud, king of Geshur. And David mourned for his son every day. So Absalom fled, and went to Geshur, and was there three years. And the soul of king David longed to go forth unto Absalom: for he was comforted concerning Amnon, seeing he was dead."

Could Amnon's death have been avoided? Surely, it could have. Two years had gone by and David hadn't done anything. Was Absalom justified in having Amnon killed? The answer would be not at all. In the end, Tamar never married, so killing Amnon did not change anything about Tamar's life. I guess if there is one consolation, it would be the fact that Amnon never had the opportunity to rape another woman.

If there is one take away from the lives of Tamar and Amnon, it would be we should always consider the consequences of our actions. What may be a temporary moment of satisfaction or pleasure for you, could be a lifetime of pain and misery for someone else. I believe God will heal and mend anyone who has endured this type of violation. Please know your life is not limited to any traumatic experience you have endured. God will cause all things to work together for your good.

We know that Absalom's actions were in response to David's inaction toward his daughter's assault. Whether it was out of guilt or neglect, David's handling of the situation was wrong, and the blood of his son was on his hands.

"The rape of Tamar by her half-brother Amnon was a tragic event that shook the house of David. The tragic story of Tamar sheds light on one specific problem that confronted the royal family of Judah. Tamar's story is a story of rape and revenge, the failure of a father to punish his son and his inability to sympathize with the plight of his violated daughter.

The rape of Tamar must be understood in light of the aftermath of David's adultery with Bathsheba and the words of divine judgment pronounced upon David and his family by the prophet Nathan. Thus, this tragedy begins to fulfill what the prophet Nathan had predicted would occur with David and his family.

After Nathan rebuked David for his sin, he announced God's judgment on David and his house: "Now therefore the sword shall never depart from your house, for you have despised me, and have taken the wife of Uriah the Hittite to be your wife. Thus says the LORD: I will raise up trouble against you from within your own house; and I will take your wives before your eyes, and give them to your neighbor, and he shall lie with your wives in the sight of this very sun. For you did it secretly, but I will do this thing before all Israel, and before the sun" (2 Samuel 12:10–12).

The sin of David's adultery with Bathsheba brought intensive emotional distress to people around David. Earl D. Bland provides a psychological evaluation of Tamar's rape and its effects on David's family. He wrote:

It is not difficult to imagine the destructive emotional and relational dynamics that must have plagued David's family during the tragedy of Tamar's rape and the subsequent killing of her assailant and half-brother Amnon by her brother Absalom. The powerful needs and expressions of rage in this narrative evoke both sorrow and outrage authenticating the scriptural portend that the sins of the father will be visited upon the children (Numbers 14:18). Amnon's lustful and violent bedding of Tamar echo's their father David's scandalous assignation with Bathsheba and the subsequent murder of her husband to cover the crime. Unified in their unhinged passion, both father and son give play to their desire beyond reasonable boundaries (2010:143).

The rape of Tamar occurred, in part, because David was deceived and betrayed by his own sons. In his desire to have sex with his half-sister Tamar, Amnon, with the help of his cousin Jonadab, devised a scheme to bring Tamar to his house.

The plan was for Amnon to deceive his father David by pretending to be sick and by requesting that his father allow Tamar to come to his house and prepare food for him. So convincing was the deception that when Amnon presented his request to his father, David did not suspect the intentions of his son, So, he allowed Tamar to go to Amnon's house and prepare food for him.

The tragedy of what happened to Tamar was made worse by the action or lack of action by David. When David heard, what Amnon had done to his sister, "he became very angry, but he would not punish his son

Amnon, because he loved him, for he was his firstborn" (2 Samuel 13:21).
Source: Claude Mariottini, Emeritus Professor of Old Testament

One of the glaring questions I have is—how did the men and women in the Bible prior to Jesus deal with their personal issues? We are familiar with David and the different issues he was confronted with. However, we never see David taking the time to heal. We understand his rejection issues with his father and brothers, but how much of an impact did that have on his parenting skills when it came to his own children?

When we look back over the life of David, his inability to discipline and deal with his sons was a major area of weakness. Unfortunately for Tamar, her father never took the opportunity or had the opportunity to heal. I pray that every broken person find their place of healing so that we can stop the cycle of brokenness.

The question remains the same. Am I my brother's keeper? The answer remains the same— yes.

SAUL AND DAVID

1 Samuel 16:1

And the LORD said unto Samuel, how long wilt thou mourn for Saul, seeing I have rejected him from reigning over Israel? fill thine horn with oil, and go, I will send thee to Jesse the Bethlehemite: for I have provided me a king among his sons.

Saul was the son of a mighty man of power by the name of Kish. It was said of Saul that there was not a more handsome person than he was among the children of Israel. From his shoulders up, he was taller than any of the people. When we first meet Saul, his father is sending him on a mission to find the family's donkeys. It's unclear if Saul was standing among the people when they petitioned God for a king, but what we do know is he was obedient to his father. I believe God had to get Saul away from his family and the people so that He could silence the voices of those around him. It is during this time that Saul encounters Prophet Samuel, and he is told that his father is no longer concerned about the donkeys; instead, he's now concerned about his son being gone for so long. However, Samuel convinces Saul to stay with him for an evening meal, after which he was to anoint Saul as King over Israel. God told Samuel that Saul was coming to look for the donkeys, but that he was the one to reign over Israel.

After reading about Saul's encounter with Samuel, your prophetic antennas should be tingling. We know that the steps of a good man are ordered by the Lord. I pray the Lord begins to awaken you to the possibilities of what He has called you to, and that as you go forth, He will direct your steps.

David was the youngest of the eight sons of Jesse, a farmer, and sheep breeder of the Israelite tribe of Judah. David likely spent much of his boyhood tending his family's sheep. We don't hear anything about David venturing outside of his hometown until his father sends him to check on his brothers at the battlefront and to take them food. The Bible makes mention that David would minister to the Lord in song while he tended to his father's sheep. It was during his time in the field that he perfects his skills. David spent much of his time to himself. I believe he grew in his sensitivity towards God as he worshiped to the Lord.

How do you handle your alone time when there isn't anyone there to reassure you of God's promises? How do you minister to the Lord? Do you take advantage of your alone time to work on certain skill sets in your life, or do you work on your shortcomings? I promise you won't always be alone.

One day, David is summoned from the fields by the Prophet Samuel, who anoints him king of Israel; this took place while Saul was still king. I'm sure David thought that he finally had something to look forward to. At last, he would get to leave the field. But to his disappointment, his father sends him back out into the fields. David was left to wrestle with the possibilities of what it would be like to be king over Israel, but as time went on, he eventually focused on the task at hand: protecting the sheep.

The story of Saul and David isn't as uncommon as many would think. Their type of interaction happens across all spectrums of relationships. Saul was chosen by God to be the first king of Israel. I believe God knew Saul really wasn't going to take heed to His instructions, but God was willing to give Saul a chance. I believe Saul was kingly material, even though when Samuel came to anoint Saul as king, he was hiding among the equipment. He remained humble among the people. He inquired of Samuel for direction and didn't move without Samuel's input. Saul maintained a good report during the beginning of his reign. He was off to a great start; he did everything that was asked of him.

However, it didn't take long for Saul to realize the benefits that came with being the king. Saul started out as a great king. He went out to battle and was victorious on Israel's behalf, plus, he was able to bring the tribes back together that had been scattered throughout Israel, thereby winning the respect and admiration of the people of Israel. Like a lot of men and women, once they have secured their positions, they don't believe there's anything that can remove them from their positions except for death, that is.

Everything seemed to be going well for Saul until he disobeyed God regarding King Agag. Saul came to the place where he thought his title of king exempted him from obeying God. He thought he could change God's instructions and not suffer the consequences of his actions. Saul had come to a place where he needed to be honored before the people of Israel. He didn't focus on his disobedience to God, but he focused on Samuel standing with him to give Israel the illusion that God was pleased with the way he'd handled the battle at Agag.

God was very specific with His instructions to Saul regarding the commandments he was given concerning his kingship over Israel. Somewhere along the way, Saul either forgot or decided not to regard God's instructions. Although Samuel told Saul that the kingdom had been stripped from him, he didn't realize that God was already in the process of choosing a new king. Saul was given more than one opportunity to obey God's instructions, but he couldn't keep his word. Once Saul came into power, it was hard for him to let it go; the more he tried to hold on to it, the more it evaded him.

It was never God's intention for Israel to have a king at the time they requested one. He wanted to be their King Himself until He was ready to give them the king He had chosen. Imagine rejecting God as King and choosing a man to be king over you instead. I'm not sure if Israel understood that there was no one greater king than God, after all, who or what could stand against Him? It was obvious that Israel really didn't know the God they served, and their need to have a king like all the other nations was such an affront to God. The kingdom has been stripped from Saul, and now here comes Goliath to confront the Israelites.

By the time Goliath came along, Saul was no longer as confident in his ability as he previously had been before the kingdom was stripped from him. He was willing to give his armor away to anyone who would take it. At this point, Saul is hiding again, only this time, he is hiding in the palace. Goliath is challenging Israel daily to send someone out to fight with him. Whereas, before Saul would have gone out to battle, but he is now hiding in the palace, and the people of Israel have begun to follow suit and hide just like their king.

On the other side of the kingdom, Samuel is getting ready to anoint David as the next king over Israel, but instead of hiding in the equipment like Saul, David has been sent by his father to the fields to tend to the sheep. David didn't have much interaction with his father and brothers. He was used to having time alone with God. As a matter of fact, when Samuel came to Jesse's house to anoint David as king, Samuel thought Jesse only had seven sons because David hadn't been invited to eat with Samuel, the Prophet. Samuel had to ask Jesse if he had another son, because he knew the one God told him about wasn't present.

Saul was searching for his father's donkeys when he met Samuel. That's when Samuel anointed Saul as king. On the other hand, we see the opposite with David. David was tending to his father's sheep out in the fields. I've heard different teachings as to why David's father didn't include him in the meeting with Samuel. From what we understand, David may have had a different mother as the other sons, and Jesse was trying to hide his indiscretions. David more than likely dealt with rejection because of having to spend most of his time alone in the fields tending his father's sheep. I think this speaks to some of the shortcomings David exhibited in his life and him feeling like he didn't measure up.

I believe David received his boldness to fight Goliath after Samuel anointed him as king. God knew before David was born what he was called to do in the Earth. Now, God had to get David to understand the significance of the call on his life. Saul didn't think there was anything that qualified him to be king over Israel. Although David appeared to have accepted his call to kingship after Samuel laid hands on him, the difference between them is that Saul was groomed by his family, while David was not. God had to use Saul's son, Jonathan, to introduce David to royalty.

One of the things that stands out between the two of them was the fact that Saul found it difficult to repent before the Lord for his sins, while David was quick to repent before the Lord, which seems odd since it seems David got in a lot more trouble than Saul. I guess the bottom line is, it was a matter of the hearts. When we look at them both, God allows us to see the difference between the king He chose (David) and the king the people chose (Saul). God knew Israel would eventually have a king; He had already chosen the time frame in which it was going to happen. But, because of the impatience of the children of Israel, God had to allow them to see what having a king like the other nations would look like.

One of the things all believers will be tested in is their ability to handle power and authority without allowing themselves to be corrupted by them. I'm of the opinion that our initial answer would be no, not me, but upon closer inspection of my own heart, I'm not sure how difficult it would be for me. Once Saul settled into his office of king, it took years to pry it out of his hands, even after God took the kingdom from him. However, David didn't force his kingship on the people of Israel, even though he knew he was God's chosen king over Israel. David had two sons who attempted to take the kingdom from their father. Most kings would have put their sons to death, but not David; he trusted God to secure his kingdom.

We all understand that there are benefits that come with power and authority, but we must be mindful of the fact that God will always be the final authority, and He will always have ultimate power. When Saul went to see the witch at Endor to seek guidance from her, it was obvious at that moment that he knew the hand of God was no longer with him. I just don't understand what he thought she could do once God had spoken. Did he think she had a way to reverse what God had spoken? We are aware of the fact that Saul could have had longevity as the king of Israel, however, he couldn't follow the instructions given to him by God. Instead, he focused more on pleasing the people than pleasing God. He became drunk on the power and authority he wielded as king, and it cost him his kingdom.

The moral of the story is—the people of God should never allow one another to serve while drunk on power. Am I my brother's keeper? Absolutely!

James and John

When we read the different gospel accounts of James and John, it can be a little confusing. In the gospel of Matthew, Jesus is walking by the seashore and calls James and John to follow Him. There is no mention of the miracle of the fish. When we meet James and John in the gospel of Mark, they are asking Jesus to allow them to sit on His right and left hand. Once again, there is no mention of the miracle of the fish. In the gospel of Luke, we learn that James and John are partners of Simon Peter, and they were there to help Simon with the load of fish that miraculously appeared in his net, and it is at this point they chose to follow Jesus. I find it odd that there is no mention of James in the gospel of John. We know that they are brothers, but why didn't John mention himself or his brother? All the same, why didn't he mention the load of fish?

From Jesus' description of James and John, sons of thunder, we get the overall picture that initially, they weren't as compassionate towards others as Jesus was. Their tolerance for those that were different from them was borderline bigoted, but at the same time, they were called by Jesus. Only Jesus knows His intent and purpose for calling James and John, however, it's not just enough for Jesus to know but for James and John to know as well. When we have a calling on our lives, we can receive all the prophetic words in the world, but if we don't embrace them and walk in them, they become unfulfilled, empty words. The truth of the matter is, as with James and John, there will be different aspects of our journeys with Christ, but the true unveiling will be in God's timing. Never allow opposition in one point of your journey to keep you from pressing forward into the next level of your journey. We can no longer see our calling as just gifts and talents, we must see our calling as an opportunity to partner with the Kingdom of Heaven to bring the Kingdom of God into the Earth.

James and John started out a little rough, but after spending time with Jesus, we slowly see them grow into the men of God that Jesus knew they were. Since Jesus knows our end from the beginning, don't allow your present circumstances and situations to make you believe that what you have now is all you will accomplish in life. You are due a fullness of time with God, where everything in life comes into alignment with God's timing and your Kairos moment presents itself.

The world is genuinely in need of those called by God to step into a particular sector of our society and help facilitate change. I believe God has called us, His children, to be change-agents in the Earth. If you find yourself wrestling with what you are called to do, I suggest you start to think slightly outside of the box. Don't overlook the possibility that you may be called to one of the seven mountains in our society. You may have done one thing all your life, but when Jesus comes knocking on your door to let you know that He has something different for you, please heed the call.

God has a way of uncovering and stirring up gifts you never knew you had. We have all seen individuals who always moved with the mainstream until an action or an event triggered them to get involved and help make changes in an area they were compassionate about. They were content to stand on the sidelines, cheer others on and go about their normal routines in life. The time is coming when God is requiring a return on His investment. When He walks past your boat and says "follow me," in that moment, your assignment is to just follow.

Matthew 4:21-22 (KJV)
"And going on from there he saw two other brothers, James the son of Zebedee and John his brother, in the boat with Zebedee their father, mending their nets, and he called them. Immediately they left the boat and their father and followed him."

Most people know that Jesus and John, the Baptist, were second cousins, but I am not sure if many know that the Apostles James and John were Jesus' first cousins. Jesus found James and John in the middle of their profession. The thing is they were not looking for Jesus, but Jesus was looking for them. There is a fullness of time when it comes to the timing of God for our lives. Sometimes, we convince ourselves that if we are not positioned in a certain place by a certain time, we will miss our destinies in Christ. This would be true if it were up to us to make it happen. However, there is a process God takes us through to prepare us for our destinies. When the time is right, He comes looking for us.

We find James and John on a fishing boat with their father, Zebedee, mending their nets after a long day of work. I am sure this day was no different than any other day for this family. More than likely, Zebedee is training his sons to one day take over the family fishing business. But on this day, they are about to have a fullness of time moment with Jesus. James and John had no way of knowing their lives were about to change so drastically, and as a result, they would be known throughout history as apostles of Jesus.

After James and John had walked with Jesus for some time, their mother, Salome, saw an opportunity and decided that she needed to secure her sons' futures with Jesus. By doing so, she would secure her future as well. The Jewish people were under the impression that Jesus came to establish a physical kingdom on Earth. We can understand why they would think such a thing. Throughout Jewish history, when God would send a deliverer to deliver His people from an evil king, such as the one they found themselves subjected to at that time, God would raise up a king from among His own people. The Jewish people thought Jesus was there to overthrow the Roman government and establish His kingdom on Earth. Jesus knew His kingdom was not of this world and would not allow the people to force Him to establish an Earthly kingdom. Salome wanted her sons to sit on the left and right hand of Jesus on His throne. Truthfully speaking, she wanted to be honored among the people. Her request appeared to be more about herself, rather than her sons.

While traveling with Jesus on a trip to Jerusalem, they needed to find a place to stay. They chose a village where there were Samaritans, but the Samaritans were not friendly towards them and did not welcome them there. James and John became very upset because of the way they'd treated Jesus and wanted to call down fire from Heaven to consume them. Jesus let them know they had the wrong spirit, after all, He had not come to destroy men's lives, but to save their lives. From that moment forward, they were known as the sons of thunder.

James and John started with Jesus in the very beginning of His ministry, and they walked close with him throughout His three years of ministry. That was until He was arrested by the Sanhedrin. They were there on the mountain of transfiguration and got to see Jesus in His transformed state as He spoke with Moses and Elias. They were among His closest friends.

We know that James and John were a part of Jesus' inner circle. They were with Him for most of the major events and moments in His life. I'm sure that when Jesus called the brothers to follow Him, they felt like they had hit the jackpot. After all, this is the Son of God. Who wouldn't want to walk close to Jesus? However, in their haste to say yes, the question one must ask is did they sit down and count the cost? It's obvious they weren't aware of what it was going to cost them to walk with Jesus. Of course, we get to read their story after the events have taken place, but they had to walk it out in real life. As they continued to walk with Jesus, the more reality began to set in.

I can genuinely say that James and John were ordained to be Jesus' apostles. Although they were ordained to walk with Jesus, that didn't prevent them from going through difficulties and struggles. I believe if we have challenges in ministry, we sometimes automatically think we have missed God, or we think we must be in the wrong church. It's important that we not allow our hardships to cause us to abdicate the calling on our lives. Please know that you are in good company. We should allow the difficulties we have endured to challenge us to go deeper into what we are called to do. For instance, if I'm called to teach, I should gather different resources to help me gain a solid foundation for teaching. I'm a true believer in the anointing, but I can testify that when you are ministering and the anointing is present, having a firm foundation on what you are ministering from the Word of God brings a level of authority that is absent when no revelation is present. We know that Jesus both taught and demonstrated what He taught.

Walking with those in leadership is not for the faint of heart. One of the most ignored scriptures in the Word of God is, "Be sober, be vigilant; because your adversary the devil, as a roaring lion, walketh about, seeking whom he may devour" (1 Peter 5:8). Satan will try to cause offense between you and your leaders; this is so that he can keep you from reaching your full potential in God. Let's not be ignorant of the devices of Satan. The Word also tells us, "Beloved, think it not strange concerning the fiery trial, which is to try you, as though some strange thing happened unto you: But rejoice, inasmuch as ye are partakers of Christ's sufferings; that, when his glory shall be revealed, ye may be glad also with exceeding joy" (1 Peter 4:12–13).

James and John had a lot to learn about leadership, and so do we. It's not up to us to determine what the journey is supposed to look like. We make ourselves available to ensure that the journey happens. What must happen before we are equipped to walk with those in leadership? We should allow the Word of God to examine our intents and motives for wanting to walk closely with leadership. Additionally, we may be surprised at what we find. We will know when we are ready to walk with those in leadership; this is when we ourselves are focused on our assignments as opposed to focusing on someone else's assignment.

> "In chapter 9 we saw the apostles arguing over who would be the "greatest" and Jesus admonished them not to confuse spiritual with worldly greatness. Apparently, they didn't heed him because now two — James and John, the brothers — go behind the others' backs to get Jesus to promise them the best spots in heaven.
> First, they try to get Jesus to agree to do for him "whatsoever" they desire — a very open-ended request that Jesus is smart enough not to fall for (curiously, Matthew has their mother make this request — perhaps to relieve James and John of the burden of this act). When he finds out exactly what they want, he tries to dissuade them by alluding to the trials he will endure — the "cup" and "baptism"

here are not meant literally but are rather references to his persecution and execution.

We're not sure that the apostles understand what he means — it's not as though they have ever displayed much perceptiveness in the past — but they insist that they are prepared to go through whatever Jesus himself will go through. Are they really ready? That's not clear, but Jesus' comments might be meant to look like a prediction of James' and John's martyrdom.

The other ten apostles, naturally, are outraged over what James and John have tried to do. They don't appreciate the brothers' going behind their backs to achieve a personal advantage. This suggests that not all was well within this group. It seems that they didn't get along all of the time and that there was infighting that was not reported.

Jesus, however, uses this occasion to repeat his earlier lesson about how a person who wants to be "great" in the kingdom of God must learn to be the "least" here on Earth, serving all others and putting them ahead of one's own needs and desires. Not only are James and John rebuked for seeking their own glory, but the rest are rebuked for being jealous of this.

Everyone is displaying the same bad character traits, just in different ways. As before, there is the problem with the sort of person who behaves in such a manner precisely in order to obtain greatness in heaven — why would they be rewarded?

Jesus on Politics

This is one of the few occasions where Jesus is recorded as having much to say about political power — for the most part, he sticks to religious issues. In chapter 8 he spoke against being tempted by the "leaven of the Pharisees...and of the leaven of Herod," but when it comes to specifics he has always focused on the problems with the Pharisees.

Here, however, he is speaking more specifically of the "leaven of Herod" — the idea that in the traditional political world, everything is about power and authority. With Jesus, however, it's all about service and ministering. Such a critique of traditional forms of political power would also serve as a critique of some of the ways in which Christian churches have been set up. There, too, we often find "great ones" who "exercise authority upon" others.

Note the use of the term "ransom" here. Passages like this have given rise to the "ransom" theory of salvation, according to which Jesus' salvation was meant as a blood payment for the sins of humanity. In a sense, Satan has been allowed dominion over our souls but if Jesus pays a "ransom" to God as a blood sacrifice, then our slates will be wiped clean."
Source: Request of James and John to Jesus by Austin Cline

James and John give us hope. There is nothing too hard for God. It does not matter what we lack in terms of our character, behaviors, and integrity, once we submit our whole self to God, there is no limit to what God can do with us. "Am I my brother's keeper?" You bet!

PETER AND ANDREW

We see another brother combo that were called to be disciples of Jesus: Simon Peter and his brother, Andrew. I find it interesting that Jesus would choose two sets of brothers. Not only were they brothers, but all four of them were fishermen. This now begs the question, what is it about fishermen that drew Jesus to them? Maybe they understood the art of fishing. For example, when you throw your net into the sea and catch a variety of fish, you must sort them out to see which ones to keep and which ones to throw back. We know that Jesus told Simon Peter and Andre, "Follow me and I will make you a fisher of men."

Andrew, Simon Peter's brother, was a disciple of John, the Baptist, before he became the first disciple of Jesus. It was also Andrew who introduced his brother, Simon, to Jesus. After becoming a disciple of Jesus, there isn't a lot mentioned about Andrew. However, Andrew was the disciple who pointed out the little boy with the five loaves and two fish. Later in his ministry, he is known as a missionary to many countries. Historical records tell us that Andrew suffered a lot as a Christian and preached for two days before dying on a cross.

As brothers, it appears that Simon Peter's personality overshadowed the personality of his brother, Andrew. Simon was known as impetuous, meaning acting or done quickly with little or inadequate thought. We could see this in his walk with Christ. Simon was somewhat of a reminder of James and John in how he was always ready to jump into action. When I think about the twelve disciples Jesus chose, it causes me to wonder what Jesus' mindset was in how He chose us. Most of us have heard in one form or another that we were sent into the Earth with a specific assignment on our lives. It would be nice if we had memory of the conversation before we left Heaven. But the truth is, as we mediate on God's Word day and night, I believe He will unfold to us our purpose for being here.

Like James and John, everything about the lives of Simon and Andrew was about to change the day Jesus called them to follow Him. I'm not sure if Simon's answer was immediate since he was married. His answer wouldn't only affect him but his wife as well. From the moment John, the Baptist, pointed out Jesus as the Lamb of God who takes away the sins of the world, Andrew was all in. There was no wife or children to consider. He was free to follow Jesus wherever He went. Simon was the only disciple of Jesus who was married, but he was also the most outspoken among them.

The Word of God tells us, "I want you to live as free of complications as possible. When you're unmarried, you're free to concentrate on simply pleasing the Master. Marriage involves you in all the nuts and bolts of domestic life and in wanting to please your spouse, leading to so many more demands on your attention. The time and energy that married people spend on caring for and nurturing each other, the unmarried can spend in becoming whole and holy instruments of God. I'm trying to be helpful and make it as easy as possible for you, not make things harder. All I want is for you to be able to develop a way of life in which you can spend plenty of time together with the Master without a lot of distractions" (1 Corinthians 7:33-34 MSG).

If the brothers were anything like most of us, they didn't always get along with one another. I would imagine this was also present among the brothers as well. At the same time, there had to be a level of comfort for them knowing that they had one another to lean on when we consider that all these men left everything to follow Jesus. I suppose there must have been times when Simon and Andrew wondered if they had made the right decision, after all, there was no laid-out plan; they had to move as Jesus moved. Jesus didn't keep them in their hometown; they traveled to places they weren't familiar with and beyond their comfort zones.

As Jesus was walking beside the Sea of Galilee, he saw two brothers, Simon called Peter and his brother Andrew. They were casting a net into the lake, for they were fishermen. "Come, follow me," Jesus said, "and I will send you out to fish for people." At once they left their nets and followed him. Matthew 4:18-22 (NIV)

Andrew and Peter were fishermen called by Jesus to follow Him. However, I am not sure how many are aware that Andrew was initially a follower of John, the Baptist. Andrew was aware of who Jesus was long before he talked his brother, Simon Peter, into coming to see the Lord. Andrew was present when John, the Baptist, pointed out Jesus as the Lamb of God who takes away the sins of the world. Although Andrew encountered Jesus before his brother, it was Simon Peter who became part of Jesus' inner core. Scripture teaches us that Peter, James, and John traveled with Jesus everywhere He went. Although Peter and Andrew are brothers, they could not have been more diverse in their personalities.

When Jesus encountered the brothers for the first time, they had just finished an unproductive day of fishing. They were mending their nets and preparing to call it a day. Jesus approached them and asked to use their boat. Understandably, the brothers were disappointed having not caught any fish after a long day of work. Jesus persisted and they agreed. I believe Jesus wanted to thank them for the use of their boat, but most importantly, He wanted to give them a glimpse into who He is. Most of us probably would have responded to Jesus the same way Simon Peter responded; he said (in so many words), "I have been at this all-night; trust me, there is nothing out there."

There must have been something in Jesus' voice that convinced them to cast their net one more time. We can attest to the fact that after moments of having tried on numerous occasions to accomplish a task and failing, the last thing we wanted to do was try again. It took faith on the brothers' part to take Jesus at His Word, and their faith was rewarded. At this point, I am sure it did not take much for Jesus to convince them to follow Him.

Luke 5:1–11 reads, "While Jesus was standing by the lake of Gennesaret, many people pushed to get near Him. They wanted to hear the Word of God. Jesus saw two boats on the shore. The fishermen were not there because they were washing their nets. Jesus got into a boat that belonged to Simon. Jesus asked him to push it out a little way from land. Then He sat down and taught the people from the boat. When He had finished speaking, He said to Simon, 'Push out into the deep water. Let down your nets for some fish.' Simon said to Him,' Teacher, we have worked all night and we have caught nothing. But because You told me to, I will let the net down.' When they had done this, they caught so many fish, their net started to break. They called their friends who were working in the other boat to come and help them. They came and both boats were so full of fish that they began to sink. When Simon Peter saw it, he got down at the feet of Jesus. He said, 'Go away from me, Lord, because I am a sinful man.' He and all those with him were surprised and wondered about the many fish. James and John, the sons of Zebedee, were surprised also. They were working together with Simon. Then Jesus said to Simon, 'Do not be afraid. From now on you will fish for men.' When they came to land with their boats, they left everything and followed Jesus."

The first question that comes to mind is, do they have any idea what they are about to get into? Major life decisions will have to be considered and family discussions will have to be had. Your whole world can change with two words; they are: follow me. You have to admire their willingness to drop everything and follow Jesus, not knowing where He would lead them. Second thought—maybe, anything would be better than fishing all night and catching nothing. To have to be a fisherman for the rest of their lives may have influenced their decision.

When Jesus found Peter and Andrew, they were casting their nets into the lake, for they were fishermen. "He said to them, 'Follow Me, and I will make you fishers of men.' At once they left their nets and followed Him."

When Jesus finds Peter and Andrew, they are busy with daily life. They were making a living and providing for their families. Note: many families in that part of the ancient world depended on fishing for their livelihood. They may have been struggling with problems. Perhaps, they had lost a share of the fish market. Perhaps, they had large families who needed supporting. Perhaps, they were having problems with their employees. However, regardless of what was taking place in their lives, Peter and Andrew stepped out on faith and followed Jesus. It is understood that the life of a fisherman was one of hardships and struggle. There is no guarantee of success, no matter how hard you try. But when it comes to providing for your family and loved ones, we should be willing to make the sacrifice. As an observer through the Word of God, it was an opportunity of a lifetime to be chosen to walk with God in the flesh and to be trained to carry His Word to the world. Of course, they had no way of knowing, at the time, how their lives would impact the world.

When we look at the life and calling of Peter and Andrew, we see how discipleship works from Jesus' perspective. Jesus was very intentional in regards to the development of His disciples. Watching Jesus transform the lives of His disciples in spite of their different personalities and the rough edges that had to be smoothed out is a miracle within itself, to say the least. By the time Jesus went to be with the Father, the foundation had been set and ready to build upon.

Jesus basically took twelve strangers minus one and formed a vehicle that could carry His plans for humanity to the world. Jesus did not choose the ones the world's system would have considered the most likely to succeed. Rather, He chose the ones who, once transformed, would be difficult to believe. The established church referred to the disciples as ignorant and unlearned, but they had to take note that they had been with Jesus.

The question we must ask ourselves is—what is it about our lives that makes others look at us and take notes that we have been with Jesus? The disciples were able to do the works that Jesus did, therefore, when the religious leaders saw the disciples, they saw Jesus. Although Jesus is not here with us physically as He was with the disciples, we know that Jesus resides on the inside of us. It's Christ in me who is the hope of glory. He left the Holy Spirit to lead us and guide us into all truth. The Holy Spirit would speak of Jesus and declare His Word unto us.

Jesus gave us the same invitation that He gave to all His disciples: "follow me and I will make you fishers of men." The Message Bible gives us one of the best exegeses of Matthew 11:28-30; it reads, "Are you tired? Worn out? Burned out on religion? Come to me. Get away with me and you'll recover your life. I'll show you how to take a real rest. Walk with me and work with me—watch how I do it. Learn the unforced rhythms of grace. I won't lay anything heavy or ill-fitting on you. Keep company with me and you'll learn to live freely and lightly."

Jesus understood that His time with the disciples was very limited, and He wanted to make sure they were well prepared for the assignment they were called to do. That's why He commanded them to wait in the upper room until they were endued with power from on high. He knew there was more they needed to receive before He could fully release them into their ministries. Holy Spirit was going to take up where He left off.

"But when the truth-giving Spirit comes, he will unveil the reality of every truth within you. He won't speak on his own, but only what he hears from the Father, and he will reveal *prophetically* to you what is to come. He will glorify me on the Earth, for he will receive from me what is mine and reveal it to you" (John:13-14 The Passion Translation).

"Luke 5:1-11 reads, 'While Jesus was standing by the lake of Gennesaret, many people pushed to get near Him. They wanted to hear the Word of God. Jesus saw two boats on the shore. The fishermen were not there because they were washing their nets. Jesus got into a boat which belonged to Simon. Jesus asked him to push it out a little way from land. Then He sat down and taught the people from the boat.

When He had finished speaking, He said to Simon, 'Push out into the deep water. Let down your nets for some fish.' Simon said to Him, 'Teacher, we have worked all night and we have caught nothing. But because You told me to, I will let the net down.' When they had done this, they caught so many fish, their net started to break. They called to their friends working in the other boat to come and help them. They came and both boats were so full of fish they began to sink. When Simon Peter saw it, he got down at the feet of Jesus. He said, 'Go away from me, Lord, because I am a sinful man.' He and all those with him were surprised and wondered about the many fish. James and John, the sons of Zebedee, were surprised also. They were working together with Simon. Then Jesus said to Simon, 'Do not be afraid. From now on you will fish for men.' When they came to land with their boats, they left everything and followed Jesus.

Luke 4:18-22 states, 'When Christ began to preach, he began to gather disciples, who should be hearers, and afterwards preachers of his doctrine, who should be witnesses of his miracles, and afterwards testify concerning them. He went not to Herod's court, not to Jerusalem, among the chief priests and the elders, but to the sea of Galilee, among the fishermen. The same power which called Peter and Andrew, could have wrought upon Annas and Caiaphas, for with God nothing is impossible. But Christ chooses the foolish things of the world to confound the wise. Diligence in an honest calling is pleasing to Christ, and it is no hindrance to a holy life. Idle people are more open to the temptations of Satan than to the calls of God. It is a happy and hopeful thing to see children careful of their parents, and dutiful."

When Christ comes, it is good to be found doing. Am I in Christ? is a very needful question to ask ourselves; and, next to that, Am I in my calling? They had followed Christ before, as common disciples, John 1:37; now they must leave their calling. Those who would follow Christ aright, must, at his command, leave all things to follow him, must be ready to part with them. This instance of the power of the Lord Jesus encourages us to depend upon his grace. He speaks, and it is done."

Source: Matthew Henry's Concise Commentary

We must understand that there is a level of sacrifice required when we genuinely take up our crosses to follow Jesus. What should that sacrifice look like? We naturally associate our time and money with sacrifice; however, I believe Jesus wants us to sacrifice our opinions, our judgments, our unhealthy emotions and our bad attitudes. We also must sacrifice our offenses along with our hurt feelings. It's time to lay it all on the altar.

How exciting it must have been for the disciples, one day you are ordinary men with ordinary lives going about your ordinary day, and then Jesus appears on the scene and everything about your life is about to change. Their names and acts will be known throughout eternity as the ones who turned the world upside down. Follow me and I will make you fishers of men.

Jesus had the disciples to wait in the upper room until they were endued with power from on high. He knew they would need help to carry out the great commission they were entrusted with. But He also told them He wouldn't leave them comfortless; it was time for the Holy Spirit to make His entrance into the Earth. John 16:14–15 reads, "He will glorify me because it is from me that he will receive what he will make known to you. All that belongs to the Father is mine. That is why I said the Spirit will receive from me what, he will make known to you." I believe Jesus would have us walk in great expectation with our hearts full of faith that, one day, He will show up on our paths with that great commission to follow Him, and like the disciples, we should be able to say, "We have left all to follow you."

Our question remains, "Am I my brother's keeper?" No doubt!

MARY AND MARTHA

The average Christian is familiar with the story of Mary and Martha, and let's not forget their brother, Lazarus. It's interesting that prior to Jesus visiting the small village where Mary and Martha lived, they had no relationship with Jesus whatsoever. So, what was it about Jesus that would cause Mary and Martha to invite Him and His disciples into their home? Obviously, they must have heard rumors about Jesus around the village, and when the opportunity presented itself, they took full advantage of it. From scripture, we can ascertain that they were written in the volume of Jesus' book and it was ordained that they would meet.

There are times when God presents us with an opportunity to connect with something or someone that can give us a different perspective other than the one we have always had. God will use people to help us connect to new seasons, new locations, and different friendships. However, for me personally, all these scenarios were difficult. Change didn't come easy for me; we can become stuck in one area of life, not realizing God is multidimensional. I would have to say because I'm a watcher, I was familiar with the spiritual aspect of a watchman, but one day, it dawned on me that a watchman can be discerning in any arena of life. I could sit back and watch interpersonal relationships and observe their interactions with one another, and it would tell me everything I needed to know about them, good or bad.

However, this was a false positive because I never allowed myself the opportunity to engage with the individuals.

Keep in mind that, as someone who has had difficulty with change, it didn't take much for me to opt out of many opportunities. It doesn't take a genius to know that I missed out on a lot of opportunities. Thinking about Mary and Martha, how great it would have been if, like Mary and Martha, I would have taken full advantage of the opportunities presented to me by God and those He sent into my life. My prayer is that you will embrace every opportunity that God presents to you and not allow any internal hindrances to sabotage your journey. There will be disappointments along the way no doubt, but don't let that stop you.

Back to Mary and Martha; they were able to place themselves in a position to become friends of Jesus and supporters of His ministry. Mary and Martha didn't insist that Jesus come to their village on a weekly basis. The sisters understood that Jesus was on a mission. When Jesus walked into their village, their entire lives were changed in that very moment. What if I told you that the same Jesus who walked into Mary and Martha's life that day in their village is the same Jesus who wants to walk into your life and change it forever? What if He wants to come and sup with you? Maybe, He's just waiting on an invitation from you. Whatever you do, don't miss your opportunity.

How does their relationship help us to understand some of the dynamics we may find in our relationships? Although Mary and Martha were sisters, their interactions with Jesus were not the same. Mary's perspective may have been, "I don't know how long this opportunity with the Messiah is going to last. Let me soak up as much knowledge as I can." Martha's perspective may have been, "This is the Messiah! I need to make sure whatever He needs while He's in my house will be provided for."

Although Jesus commended Mary for choosing the better part by sitting at His feet, He commented that Martha was busy and worried a bit too much. He didn't tell Martha to stop what she was doing and come and sit next to Mary at His feet. He just wanted Martha to not worry about her serving. How does this relate to us? It's always better to take the time to sit with Jesus and hear His heart. When we spend time with Him, it makes it easier to serve Him in whatever capacity we are called to serve in. Our service will not always look the same as someone else's service, but like Mary and Martha, we will serve based on our perspective of who He is and what He means to us.

The Word of God reads, "For the eyes of the LORD run to and fro throughout the whole Earth, to show Himself strong on behalf of *those* whose heart *is* loyal to Him" (2 Chronicles 16:9). We all should want to be found by the Lord so that He can show Himself strong on our behalves. May His light on the inside of us shine so brightly that He can't help but stop and turn aside to see whose heart is reflecting His glory.

As Jesus and his disciples were on their way, he came to a village where a woman named Martha opened her home to him. She had a sister called Mary, who sat at the Lord's feet listening to what he said.
Luke 10:38-39 (NIV)

When it comes to Mary and Martha, I get the sense Jesus was just as intentional with them as He was with the woman at the well. I must go through Bethany. The Bible tells us later why He chose to go to Bethany and the reason He needed to be there. The Bible also tells us that the sisters welcomed Him and His disciples into their home. Not only did He visit with them for a while, but He stayed long enough for Martha and Mary to establish an intimate relationship with Him. It is obvious that they made quite an impression on Him because the Word says Jesus loved Mary and Martha, and their brother, Lazarus.

Jesus needed a place to get away from the crowd and from the noise of the people. He realized that not all the people were there because they believed in Him, but because of what He could do for them. At this point, Jesus is coming to the end of His ministry and He knows He must go to Jerusalem. Once in Jerusalem, the fulfillment of His assignment starts to accelerate. It is at this time that He is anointed for His burial.

When we consider Jesus' interaction with Mary, Martha and their brother, Lazarus, it allows us to see Jesus' love for the body of Christ. I believe there are times and situations when Jesus does the same for us as He does for

Mary and Martha. He comes and visits us. We may not always recognize Him when He comes, but trust me, He is a very present help in the time of trouble. It does not matter where you find yourself, He will find you.

Sometimes, in our frustration, we expect Jesus to forget about everyone else, because surely, what we're dealing with is an emergency and we want Him to come immediately to our aid. However, there are times when Jesus allows us to trust Him in the wait. Since He knows the beginning from the end, He does not allow us to circumvent the process. When the sisters sent a message to Jesus saying their brother, Lazarus, was sick, He did not come to their home immediately. Jesus was strategic in everything He did.

> "A few months before this incident, we find Mary and Martha at a time of crisis: their brother Lazarus was dead. Jesus had gone with his disciples "beyond Jordan into the place where John at first baptized." (John 10:40.) After Lazarus's sisters sent word to Jesus, it was Martha who went out to meet him, while Mary "sat still in the house." (John 11:20.) Herein our biblical sisters teach us the need to turn to our Savior for help in our own personal crises.
>
> Here are two sisters with distinct personalities, yet both possess great faith in their Lord. Each of them separately declares the same words to Jesus: "If thou hadst been here, my brother had not died." (John 11:21, 32.) But it is Martha who expresses her faith that Jesus can yet restore life to her brother: "But I know, that even now, whatsoever thou wilt

ask of God, God will give it thee." (John 11:22.) After Jesus describes the hope of the Resurrection, Martha, who most certainly is not "cumbered" on this occasion, firmly declares her testimony as she proclaims with conviction, "Yea, Lord: I believe that thou art the Christ, the Son of God, which should come into the world." (John 11:27.)

Her faith is well placed, as attested by the astonishing experience that follows. We can only imagine the glorious scene as the grieving of those assembled to mourn the death of Lazarus turns to rejoicing when Lazarus comes forth from his grave. (See John 11:40–44.)

This, in fact, is the picture I wish I could paint. What a glorious occasion to set to canvas! It is this scene, more than any other, which most clearly illustrates the faith Mary and Martha had in the Lord.

There is a fundamental risk involved in labeling someone based upon one or two incidents in their lives. Martha has been called "practical" and Mary "spiritual." In reality both were practical, both were spiritual. Both loved and served Jesus; all three scriptural accounts illustrate this. Should not each of us desire to be somewhat like both of them?"

Source: Evelyn T. Marshall The Church Of Jesus Christ of Latter-Day Saints

Mary and Martha had no idea that God was going to use them to glorify Himself in the Earth. Their one act of welcoming Jesus into their home was the catalyst for one of the greatest miracles in the world to take place. They were able to see the goodness of the Lord in the land of the living. Once they knew who Jesus was, it didn't take much for them to be fully persuaded that if He showed up, whatever they needed would be provided. But what happens when He doesn't show up within the time frame that works best for us?

Mary and Martha were faced with that very challenge, and so will we be. How much of what we say or believe about Jesus is based on a hope and a prayer, or do we really believe what He promised us in His Word? In all honesty, I can say I believe Jesus can do all He promised in His Word, but the reality is, I'm not always sure He will do it for me. I can do all things through Christ who strengthens me. The keyword for me is "who strengthens me." However, if left to my own strength, much prayer is required. Living in a fallen world can take a toll on you. We have an enemy who's always looking to destroy us and hinder us from reaching God's purpose in the Earth.

Jesus makes the statement, "Truly I tell you, wherever this gospel is preached throughout the world, what she has done will also be told, in memory of her" (Matthew 26:13). Isn't it interesting that Jesus said that what Mary had done would be in memory of her and not of Him? Jesus was referring to Mary preparing Him for His burial. How connected to Jesus did Mary have to be that God Himself would give her that revelation and the assignment? I look forward to the day (and it is coming) when our worship unto the Lord is so pure, it causes the Heavens to open and God allows us to see Jesus in all His splendor and glory.

Based on the sister's service to Jesus, you would have thought Martha would have been the one to anoint Jesus for His burial. But when we consider how Mary leaned into His every word and didn't leave His side, God must have given her a revelation of what was about to happen to Jesus. She was willing to lay everything on the line, including her substance, her reputation, and her dignity. Her heart was sold out to Him, and Jesus rewarded her faithfulness.

What are you expecting to happen when you open your door to Jesus and welcome Him in? This has nothing to do with salvation; this is about your Father wanting to show you the expanse of His Kingdom. I would venture to say that some of the greatest adventures of your lifetime are waiting outside your door to scoop you up and take you places in the spirit you could have only dreamed about. Let's stop limiting God to what we can access with our five senses. Let God reintroduce you to your spirit man—that part of you that's made in His image and His likeness, and let the adventures begin. We should no longer be Earth-bound. Our Father has given us access to all that belongs to Him. It's time we go on an expedition in the spirit realm.

God wants the spirit realm to become normal for us, after all, we have dual citizenship. He wants to relate to us in both realms. Let's encourage one another to remove all restraints in our lives that will try to keep us Earth-bound. Jesus said nothing is impossible to him that believes. We have become so Earth-bound that we have had very little heavenly influence. Being heavenly minded is how we should navigate our earthly lives. Don't allow the enemy to cause you to shrink back from what God has made available to you because you are afraid of what others may say about you.

"This lesson is about one of Jesus' very dear friends – a man named Lazarus and his two sisters, Mary, and Martha, who lived in Bethany. Have someone read you their story in John, Chapter 11, and verses 1-45 and see if you could use a friend like Jesus too. One day, Lazarus got very sick. His sisters sent word to Jesus and told him about their brother and asked Him to come. Jesus was in another town, so He didn't come right away. When Jesus finally arrived, Martha ran to meet Him and told Him that Lazarus had died four days earlier. She was upset with Jesus that He had not come sooner to help Lazarus. She said, "If only You had been here, my brother would not have died."

Then we have the shorted verse in the Bible, "Jesus wept." (John 11: 35) Jesus was sad for his friends even though He knew what He was going to do. Jesus then told Martha, "Your brother will rise again. I am the resurrection and the life. Whoever lives and believes in Me will never die."

Martha and her sister Mary didn't understand, but they took Jesus to where Lazarus was buried. When they arrived at his tomb, Jesus said to roll away the stone that covered the entrance. He prayed to His Father and then He called out in a loud voice, "Lazarus, come out!" Lazarus then walked out of the tomb! He wasn't dead anymore or even sick! Mary and Martha were so happy to have their brother back with them.

How would you like to have a best friend like that? Well, you do! Jesus is always your friend and wants what is best for you. He'll help you and never go away from you no matter what happens in your life. He is the "bestest" kind of best friend we could ever have!"

Source: Jesus and his friend Lazarus by Ann Moody

Jesus was very intentional in the way He handled Mary, Martha, and Lazarus. How special must your family be that God would include you all in the volume of the book that was written for all the world? How special must you be for Him to declare that wherever the gospel was preached that you would be remembered? God's plan for your life far outweighs anything you can imagine for yourself. The Word of God teaches us that before we were formed in our mother's womb, God knew us. If God knew us before we were formed in our mother's womb, shouldn't we inquire of Him as to what He formed us to be and get on with it?

One of the things we learn from the story of Mary and Martha is that Jesus doesn't move in our timing, nor in the way we expect Him to come. Let's trust that Jesus has seen the book written for each of us and He's come to make sure we walk in it. The Word of God tells us that Jesus is a friend that sticks closer than a brother. He is also a friend to the friendless. The scriptures teach us that Jesus is always with us, even until the end of this age.

"Am I my brother's keeper?" With my whole heart!

THE PRODIGAL SON

I don't know about you, but there are certain aspects of the parable of the prodigal son I can identify with. For instance, desiring freedom from the mundane tasks I must do daily and just imagining what my life could be like if I only did what I wanted to do when I wanted to do it. Although the thoughts are fleeting, there's a certain satisfaction in allowing myself to daydream. When I think about the parable of the prodigal son, his father is portrayed as a man of substance and generosity, a man who listened to his sons without judgment. When Jesus speaks a parable, there's always much wisdom attached to it. My first thought is what is it about this story that depicts certain aspects of His character traits? What is Jesus trying to convey to us about His relationship with the children of God? Oftentimes, we read the Word of God like it's a novel rather than an instruction manual. We understand the topical meaning, which is obvious to the casual reader, but what's the transformational, life-changing lesson or principle Jesus wants us to walk away with?

At first glance, the son appears to be rebellious and selfish. He's in such a hurry to receive his inheritance or the portion of goods that were due to him. What I find interesting is the older brother didn't ask for anything, but the father divided his livelihood between him and his brother. If I had to make a guess, I would say, one lesson Jesus wants us to walk away with is—we can't handle everything He has for us at one time. An example of this is seen in the lives of many lottery winners, most of whom have never had to steward large amounts of money. At first, it can seem like an endless supply of cash. They quickly find that it costs to have large sums of money, and it costs to hold onto it. However, for those who deal with that level of finances on a regular basis, they are aware of the amount of responsibility that comes with maintaining and sustaining large sums of money at one time. We don't know if the son allowed himself to learn stewardship from his father.

The fact that the younger son took everything he had gives us the impression he had no intention of returning to his father's house. He got as far away from his family as he could. The Bible says he went to a far country. With his endless supply in hand, he was ready to make his mark on the world. I wonder if the prodigal son considered the fact that his father had hired servants to help him to amass his wealth. It wasn't a one-man show. Did he understand anything about systems and markets, or the need to invest his money? It makes you wonder if the younger son learned or gleaned anything from watching his father manage their household. Maybe, he felt as if his older brother was going to inherit everything anyway, so why bother learning about household management?

What happens when our plans don't work out like we thought they would? Did we take the time to count the costs to see if we had what was needed to make the plan work? When the prodigal son was in the father's house, he really didn't have to worry about anything. Everything he needed was provided by the father. Lesson two, our heavenly Father knows what we have need of before we ask. We can be guilty of treating God as if His sole purpose for saving us was to give us all the desires of our hearts, after all, if He loves us like He says He does, we think that we shouldn't lack anything. God is more interested in our growth than our pleasure. His Word tells us that He holds no good thing from those that walk uprightly; the caveat being those who walk uprightly. God is not interested in helping us consume material things upon our lusts. He wants to give us as much as we can steward.

What keeps us from running to the Father in our times of need? What do we believe about the Father that makes us think we have to earn our way back into the Father's good graces? For whatever reason, the prodigal son's view of how his father would receive him was totally different from how the father viewed his son. This speaks to the type of relationship the son had towards his father. On the other hand, the father didn't berate his son. He understood his son wasn't ready for what he so desperately desired, but he also knew that his love for his son was greater than any amount of money he could give him. Another life lesson—the father's love didn't rest in the amount of things he could give his son; the father's love rested in the fact that he was his son. As sons and daughters of God, we need to embrace that truth and be comforted in knowing that nothing can separate us from the love of God. Sometimes, it's our pride, shame or embarrassment that keeps us from running to the Father, but that was dealt with by Jesus on the cross. We are now admonished to come boldly to the throne of grace so that we may obtain mercy and find grace to help in time of need. I would say one of the main reasons some believers return to the world is they don't understand how much they are valued in the Father's eyes.

The enemy has guilt-tripped the children of God into believing that God is looking for their perfection, which is the farthest thing from the truth. God is looking for your maturity. He is very much aware that maturity is a process and it does take time. However, our obedience can help accelerate the process. When we find more comfort in the presence of those who don't know nor love God than we do in Jesus who died and gave His life for us, it's time to repent and rededicate our lives to Him. The question is why is God always the last result? Why do we have to hit rock bottom before we take Him at His Word that says He will never leave us or forsake us? I get it—we've had people make promises (male and female) that they couldn't make good on, not because they didn't want to. They just decided not to, for whatever reason. Our heavenly Father is not like man. When He says something, He makes it good.

We don't have to come to God as beggars, hoping He will feel sorry for us and have mercy on us. Our times are in His hands. He has already made provisions for any misstep or setback you will encounter in this life. Remember, He knows the number of hairs on your head, or the lack thereof. So, run to the Father and not away from Him.

Allow Him to sing over you and call a feast in your honor because His child is home. I know when you've never known the love of an Earthly father, it can be difficult to embrace a father that seems distant and aloof. But the Word of God tells us that if our mother or our father forsakes us, God Himself will take us up. In other words, God will stand in their stead. Allow God to wash away the stains of your past so that He can reveal your future to you, since it has already been written and tailor-made just for you. It's time to arise, shake yourself and be about your Father's business!

"And he said, A certain man had two sons: And the younger of them said to his father, Father, give me the portion of goods that falleth to me. And he divided unto them   his   living."
Luke 15:11-12 (KJV)

Let's define prodigal: extravagant, high-rolling, profligate, spendthrift, squandering, thriftless, unthrifty, wasteful. (Source: Merriam-Webster)

I know there are many who would say that the parable of the prodigal son is more about the father than the sons. I would agree to disagree. However, our focus here is on the sons. In most families, the older siblings feel the younger siblings get away with certain behaviors the older siblings were never allowed to get away with. Unfortunately, the older siblings must endure the learning curve of their parents, along with their trials and errors before the younger sibling comes along.

There are times when the child feels he/she has outgrown their parents' house. Usually, it is because of the parents' rules and regulations. The prodigal son, however, felt he was missing out on life. We can all attest to the fact that raising children in this society today is a whole new ball game. Parents must be able to play a mean game of chess in order to stay ahead of the enemy's every move.

Luke 15:11-32 reads, "And he said, A certain man had two sons: And the younger of them said to his father, Father, give me the portion of goods that falleth to me. And he divided unto them his living. And not many days after the younger son gathered all together, and took his journey into a far country, and there wasted his substance with riotous living. And when he had spent all, there arose a mighty famine in that land; and he began to be in want. And he went and joined himself to a citizen of that country; and he sent him into his fields to feed swine. And he would fain have filled his belly with the husks that the swine did eat: and no man gave unto him. And when he came to himself, he said, How, many hired servants of my father's, have bread enough and to spare, and I perish with hunger! I will arise and go to my father, and will say unto him, Father, I have sinned against heaven, and before thee, And am no more worthy to be called thy son: make me as one of thy hired servants. And he arose and came to his father. But when he was yet a great way off, his father saw him, and had compassion, and ran, and fell on his neck, and kissed him. And the son said unto him, Father, I have sinned against heaven, and in thy sight, and am no more worthy to be called thy son. But the father said to his servants, Bring forth the best robe, and put it on him; and put a ring on his hand, and shoes on his feet: And bring hither the fatted calf, and kill it; and let us eat, and be merry: For this my son was dead, and is alive again; he was lost, and is found. And they began to be merry. Now his elder son was in the field: and as he came and drew nigh to the house, he heard musick and dancing. And he called one of the servants and asked what these things meant. And he said unto him, Thy brother is come; and thy father hath killed the fatted calf, because he hath received him safe and sound. And he was angry and would not go in: therefore. came his father out, and intreated him. And he answering said to his father, Lo, these many years do I serve thee, neither transgressed I at any time thy commandment: and yet thou never gavest me a kid, that I might make merry with my friends: But as soon as this thy son was come, which hath devoured thy living with harlots, thou hast killed for him the fatted calf. And he said unto him, Son, thou art ever with me, and all that I have is thine. It was meet that we should make merry and be glad: for this thy brother was dead, and is alive again; and was lost, and is found."

It took the younger son going out into the world to understand the benefits of the father's house. In his father's house, there was protection, provision, and peace. He did not have to worry about food, shelter or clothing. Everything he needed was supplied by the father. He had the opportunity to see how ill-prepared he was to navigate the challenges he faced in the world because he took for granted everything his father provided for him. The older son, on the other hand, did not realize that he had access to everything in his father's house as a son. He tried to earn what his father had freely laid aside just for him to enjoy. The eldest son's insecurities caused him to accuse his father of showing favoritism to his younger brother. His lack of understanding regarding his position in his father's house caused him to approach his father as a servant. His focus was more on serving the father than enjoying his relationship with the father.

I believe God's heart is the same towards us as the father's heart was towards the prodigal son. There are times when we think we are ready to step out and do all that God has placed in our hearts to do. Anoint me, Father, confer a title upon me, and give me favor with You and man. When all the Father wants is to enjoy the journey with you. Our zeal for God is not always according to knowledge. What if the father of the prodigal son had come to him and said, "Son, I think it's time for you to experience life outside of my home?"

We must take the time to get to know Father God, especially those of us who may not fully understand the role and function of a father. Understanding the role of a father is necessary to keep us from thinking we know how to better govern our lives than the father does. I understand when some people hear the word father, there are negative connotations attached to it. Not everyone's memory of their relationship with their father is a positive one. For others, there is no memory at all since many never knew their fathers.

Yet, for others of us, we find it much easier to see God as Father based on the relationship we had with our fathers. This doesn't, by any means, infer that our relationship with our father was perfect, but there was a sense of belonging and security. There's something special about looking back over your life and seeing your father there. Not to mention, when you have certain choices or decisions to make, you will sometimes hear his voice. When my dad passed in September of 2021, it felt like a part of me had been taken away. The world doesn't feel the same without him in it.

When we look at this story from a spiritual perspective as it pertains to the church at large, we begin to get a better understanding of the role spiritual parents play in our spiritual maturity. The Word of God teaches us that, as it is in the natural, so it is in the spirit. "However, the spiritual is not first, but the natural, and afterward the spiritual" (1 Corinthians 15:46). Just as there are good parents in the natural, there are good spiritual parents out there. The same is true when it comes to abusive parents. We have them both in the natural and in the spiritual. Not all natural parents are healthy examples of what parents should look like. Neither are all spiritual parents healthy examples of what spiritual parents should look like. This is very important from both the spiritual and natural perspectives because parents are responsible for helping you grow in the things of life and in the things of God. Our relationship with our spiritual parents should be healthy and fulfilling. This does not mean they have to be perfect, but they should be healthy.

We are now going to deal with the fact that there are abusive spiritual parents in the body of Christ. Unfortunately, not everyone qualifies to parent others. We also understand that there is a learning curve and God knows parenting under any circumstance is not for the faint of heart. However, there are individuals who are unfit to parent God's people in a healthy and responsible way. We have all heard stories of abuse and molestation at the hands of those who were supposed to protect the sheep. Just a caution to church leaders—you are the under-shepherd and Jesus is the Good Shepherd who gave His life for the sheep. If He gave His life for the sheep, please be mindful that He will protect the sheep.

We do not want to overlook the truth that there are spiritual parents who have suffered much at the hands of the sheep. Not everyone who attends church has pure motives. There are those whose whole focus is to get as much as they can out of their local churches without giving anything in return. They work on the emotions of those in the church, manipulating them into giving up their resources. The sacrifices of the spiritual parents are not always met with appreciation and gratefulness. Our spiritual parents deserve our respect and support. Let's honor them as the men and women God has called them to be. It should be in the heart of every true son and daughter of God to make their spiritual parents proud.

"Spiritual abuse is not as easily identifiable. Spiritual abuse occurs when someone in the church or in a Christian organization, who has authority and therefore power, wounds a believer by the way he wields that authority. The scale of this abuse can vary from very mild to devastating.

Since spiritual abuse involves the misuse of authority to distort relations for the purposes of control, it is necessary to establish what the ultimate authority is for Christ's followers. Christ, the God who is both God and man, speaks through the Bible. The Holy Spirit, working through illumination, confirmation, and interpretation, assists the believer by guiding, comforting, and applying scriptural truth. Christ is authoritative in the believer and in Scripture. We can trust the work of God in the individual through the leading of the Holy Spirit and guidance and interpretation of several trusted believers.

A Relationship of Control

One way to recognize any kind of abuse is to examine whether the person who feels the pressure of control has the freedom to make their own decisions. Are they treated as a capable person and treated with respect? If they have no voice in a situation, there may be unhealthy kinds of control going on. (Note: in this article I am not speaking of children, or the very elderly, or those who are mentally compromised, but the average Christian person).

Many who have experienced spiritual abuse do not realize the relational pattern of control that has developed until there is a major betrayal by the

controller. Picture a family that has been deeply involved in a church, and close to the church leadership. The family makes a decision about direction for themselves, and this decision evokes disagreement from the church leadership. This family then finds themselves distanced, and on the outs socially. They lose friends, experience slander, and may even be shunned. The damage extends to their children, and they may find it impossible to trust other Christ followers or even God."
Source: Spiritual Abuse Bellevue Christian Counseling, Andrew Engstrom

Relationships are developed over time, space, and distance. If we are wise, the first relationship that should be developed after salvation is our relationship with the Father, the Son, and the Holy Spirit. Being in a relationship with the Trinity gives us a foundational structure for every other relationship we will ever enter. The Word of God teaches, "If a man says I love God, and hateth his brother, he is a liar: for he that loveth not his brother whom he hath seen, how can he love God whom he hath not seen?" (1 John 4:20). Godly relationships are important to God, therefore they should be important to us.

One of the lessons we can take away from the story of the prodigal son is—God knows when we are ready to leave the Father's house. The prodigal son gives us insight and wisdom regarding our position in Christ. There was nothing he could have done to make the father see him as a servant. He was fully restored as a son in the father's house and placed back in line to receive his full inheritance. "I no longer call you servants, because a servant does not know his master's business. Instead, I have called you friends, for everything that I learned from my Father I have made known to you" (John 15:15).

The elder son thought he needed to earn the father's favor; he didn't understand that everything that belonged to the father belonged to him. His disdain for his brother was truly unwarranted because, if nothing else, he could have enjoyed that which he resented his brother for. Let not that attitude be named among us! When our brothers rejoice, let us rejoice and when our brothers weep, let's weep with them. There are more than enough resources in the Father's house for each of His children.

"Am I my brother's keeper?" Joyfully so!

MARY AND JOSEPH

Matthew 1:18–24 KJV

"Now the birth of Jesus Christ was on this wise: When as his mother Mary was espoused to Joseph, before they came together, she was found with child of the Holy Ghost. Then Joseph her husband, being a just *man*, and not willing to make her a public example, was minded to put her away privily. But while he thought on these things, behold, the angel of the Lord appeared unto him in a dream, saying, Joseph, thou son of David, fear not to take unto thee Mary thy wife: for that which is conceived in her is of the Holy Ghost. And she shall bring forth a son, and thou shalt call his name JESUS: for he shall save his people from their sins. Now all this was done, that it might be fulfilled which was spoken of the Lord by the prophet, saying, Behold, a virgin shall be with child, and shall bring forth a son, And they shall call his name Emmanuel, which being interpreted is, God with us. Then Joseph being raised from sleep did as the angel of the Lord had bidden him, and took unto him his wife."

When we think about the family life of Jesus, we see that God doesn't try to present everything in a pretty package. I'm sure that Mary, growing up in Nazareth in the city of Galilee as a young Jewish girl, would have overheard conversations about the coming Messiah. She likely heard stories of how He would save His people from Roman bondage and set them free, and how He would be born of a virgin. The men in her village probably discussed how the

147

Messiah was soon to come. I can imagine Mary and the other young girls in the village secretly fantasizing about being chosen and what it would be like to give birth to the Messiah.

When we first meet Mary in the gospel of Matthew, she is already engaged to a man named Joseph. What happens next will change the course of history. It is believed that Mary was twelve years old when she was engaged to Joseph. The angel, Gabriel, approaches Mary and tells her that she is highly favored of the Lord and that she will bring forth the Son of God. However, in the book of Luke, we get a clearer picture of how Mary was chosen to bring forth the Messiah.

Of all the young virgins in Nazareth, Mary was chosen by God Himself to give birth to His Son. I'm sure Mary's encounter with the angel was one she would never forget, or she likely wondered if what the angel said was really going to happen. What would you do if you found out that you were highly favored of God and you were going to be the mother of the Messiah? What if there was no one in your village you could tell this secret to, not even your parents? Mary needed someone to talk to, and when she heard that Elizabeth was pregnant, she finally had someone who would understand her plight.

"In the sixth month the angel Gabriel was sent from God to a city of Galilee named Nazareth, to a virgin betrothed to a man whose name was Joseph, of the house of David. And the virgin's name was Mary. And he came to her and said, 'Greetings, O favored one, the Lord is with you!' But she was greatly troubled at the saying, and tried to discern what sort of greeting this might be. And the angel said to her, 'Do not be afraid, Mary, for you have found favor with God. And behold, you will conceive in your womb and bear a son, and you shall call his name Jesus. He will be great and will be called the Son of the Most- High. And the Lord God will give to him the throne of his father David, and he will reign over the house of Jacob forever, and of his kingdom there will be no end.' And Mary said to the angel, 'How will this be, since I am a virgin?' And the angel answered her, 'The Holy Spirit will come upon you, and the power of the Most High will overshadow you; therefore the child to be born will be called holy—the Son of God. And behold, your relative Elizabeth in her old age has also conceived a son, and this is the sixth month with her who was called barren. For nothing will be impossible with God.' And Mary said, 'Behold, I am the servant of the Lord; let it be to me according to your word.' And the angel departed from her" (Luke 1:26-38).

I don't know about you, but as a twelve-year old virgin, if I had been told I was going to give birth to the Son of God, I'm not sure I would have been as calm as Mary was. Without a shadow of doubt, Mary's life was forever changed that day, although Elizabeth was the only person she initially shared her good news with. Mary must have rejoiced within herself just thinking about who she carried in her womb. Spiritually speaking, an immaculate conception, the first and only one of its kind, was truly miraculous. However, in the natural this could look a little messy, after all, who is going to believe God got a young Jewish girl pregnant? When Mary returned from visiting

Elizabeth, her secret was out. It was obvious she was well into her pregnancy, and there was no way to hide it. As any man would be, Joseph was humiliated by the news, but he loved Mary too much to have her stoned to death. He was willing to put her away privately.

I believe Joseph was purposefully chosen by God to be Mary's husband. He knew Joseph's character and integrity, and that he was an honorable man. Joseph had to cover and protect, not only Mary, but her unborn child as well. I find it interesting that everyone in the village knew Joseph wasn't the father of Mary's child, but later in scripture, he is commonly referred to, along with Mary, as the mother and father of Jesus. Joseph raised Jesus as if He was his very own to the point that everyone else followed suit.

We know God took all of this into consideration when He chose Mary, but what must it have been like for Mary? It's interesting that the Word of God doesn't mention how Mary's parents responded to the pregnancy. Now, Mary must face her parents and I'm not sure how well, "I'm carrying the Son of God" is going to go over. As a parent, my first question would be—do you think I'm stupid? Just saying. More than likely, her parents inquired about Joseph and how he was handling the news. We know Joseph was considered a man of great means, and I'm sure the marriage was arranged in a way that Mary and her family would be well taken care of. It appears that this is no longer going to happen because of Mary. At least, he didn't have her stoned to death.

News travels fast in small towns. By now, everyone was aware that the marriage between Joseph and Mary had been called off. The question now is—who is the father of Mary's child? If their culture was anything like ours, Mary couldn't go anywhere without people staring and talking about her. Mary knew the baby in her womb was from God, and she was willing to believe that everything God spoke through the angel was going to happen. "Be it unto me according to your word." There are times in all our lives when what we are believing God for causes us to look like fools for His sake. It's in times like these that we must endure the criticism and judgment of others, all the while holding onto our belief that God is going to somehow come through for us. I believe Mary must have been quite frustrated trying to convince others of what she already knew.

It's hard to articulate the elation that floods one's soul when God comes through for you in a way you could have never imagined. You walk around as if you are dreaming. Although, you were believing God to do it, you must admit there was this small part of you that didn't think He would. When God visited Joseph in his dream, Joseph's heart must have leaped for joy, not only because he loved Mary and wanted to marry her, but also because everything she said to him was true. What if Joseph had allowed his emotions and the gossip in the village to get the better of him, and without thinking, he'd decided to have Mary stoned to death? I believe God knew Joseph's heart and character, and God knew Joseph would do the right thing. I'm sure by this time, Mary was feeling all alone, but when Joseph showed up to tell her about his dream from God, that feeling of elation must have flooded her soul and she knew from that moment forward that everything the angel said to her was going to happen.

I wonder what the parents of Mary must have thought when they realized that they were going to be the grandparents of the Son of God. By now, Joseph is beginning to understand the responsibility and the weight of what he has been entrusted to watch over and to protect. God has a way of rearranging our lives until we come into alignment with the destinies He has chosen for us. God can take our mess and create our greatest life's messages. How are you enduring and viewing the messes in your life? My prayer is that you will allow God to birth your life's message from your mess.

Most people are familiar with the birth of Christ, however, my focus in this writing is to shed light on His family's dynamics. Although Mary was married to Joseph, Joseph is not Jesus' natural father. Joseph would have been considered Jesus' stepfather today. We know that Mary and Joseph had four sons and two daughters after she gave birth to Jesus. Most stepchildren are aware of some of the differences in the way natural children are treated and the way stepchildren are treated. The thought of Jesus being a stepchild somehow takes the stigma from the word itself. From scripture reading, there is very little written of Joseph after the birth of Jesus. As a matter of fact, the last time Joseph is mentioned in scripture is when Jesus is twelve-years old and He'd stayed behind at the temple asking questions and taking questions of religious leaders.

We can assume that Jesus was Mary's favorite child, for obvious reasons, but the first reason is He's the firstborn;

the second reason is because He was given to her from God. But what about Joseph? Jesus would have been special to Joseph because God chose him to raise His Son. There can't be a greater honor than raising the Son of God. How did Jesus interact with the rest of His brothers and sisters, knowing that He was the Son of God? I'm sure, at some point, Mary had to have that conversation with Him, after all, there must have been rumors surrounding His birth. And those rumors may have affected His brothers and sisters as well. As the Son of God, at some point in His development, there must have been signs that there was something very different about Jesus. It was evident from His conversation with the religious leaders that His knowledge and understanding of the scriptures was far beyond someone who was only twelve-years old. Mary asked Jesus, "Why did you do this to us?" This was in reference to Jesus staying behind in the temple without their knowledge. We can see from her question that Mary hadn't considered the possibility that Jesus was becoming more aware of who He was. Jesus' response to Mary was, "Didn't you know I have to be about my Father's business?"

"When his parents saw him, they were astonished. His mother said to him, 'Son, why have you treated us like this? Your father and I have been anxiously searching for you" (Luke 2:48).

"Why were you searching for me?' he asked. 'Didn't you know I had to be in my Father's house?' But they did not understand what he was saying to them" (Luke 2:49-50). In this exchange, we can see the choice that Jesus felt He had to make—do I obey what I believe my Father is asking me to do or do I obey my parents and go home with them? I believe He made the honorable choice to go home with His parents. I believe had Jesus stayed in Jerusalem, He would have circumvented the process that was written in the volume of the book concerning Him. It was Jewish law that He had to be thirty-years old before He could enter His ministry. At this time, the enemy had no idea who Jesus was, but remaining in Jerusalem would have caused Him to manifest His Identity before the time. It was wisdom on the part of Mary and Joseph to take Him home. Although, we may be aware of the call and the destiny on our lives, there is a fullness of time for each of us; this is the Kairos moment when God has worked in us, both to do His will and to do His good pleasure. This is when the Father knows He can trust us to carry out the assignment according to His will and His plans. "But when the fullness of the time had come, God sent forth His Son, born of a woman, born under the law, to redeem those who were under the law, that we might receive the adoption as sons" (Galatians 4:4-5).

What was life like for Jesus? Did He have interactions with God at a young age? Did God allow the angels to visit Him in His dreams to give Him instructions and directions regarding what was about to come? When did He realize that God was His Father and not Joseph, and what impact did that have on His life? When He read the Torah, did He realize He was reading about Himself? At what point did He accept His assignment? My question to you is—what is it about Jesus' life that you can identify with? I believe there comes a time in each of our lives when we must answer some of the same questions Jesus was confronted with. Who has God placed in your life to help you reach your destiny?

What about the silent years? The scriptures don't have much to say about Jesus' life between the ages of thirteen and twenty-nine. We can speculate that, by this time, Joseph was no longer living and a lot of the responsibility to help provide for the family had fallen on Jesus and His siblings. We can assume that Joseph must have taught Jesus his carpentry skills, since the Bible refers to Jesus as a carpenter, and that was the custom at the time. I believe God intentionally kept those years silent, as my Apostle, Bryan Meadow would say. He was in His hidden season and the infancy of His gift. I would like to suggest that during our silent years, we allow God to perfect those things concerning us, so we can let patience have her perfect work, that we may be perfect and entire, wanting nothing. It's in our patience that we possess our soul.

After the silent years, we see the fully mature Son of God, "Then cometh Jesus from Galilee to Jordan unto John, to be baptized of him. But John forbad him, saying, I have need to be baptized of thee, and comest thou to me? And Jesus answering said unto him, Suffer, it to be so now: for thus it becometh us to fulfil all righteousness. Then he suffered him. And Jesus, when he was baptized, went up straightway out of the water: and, lo, the heavens were opened unto him, and he saw the Spirit of God descending like a dove, and lighting upon him: And lo a voice from heaven, saying, This, is my beloved Son, in whom I am well pleased" (Matthew 3:13-17). Jesus is now ready for His public ministry. After being baptized by John, the Baptist, Jesus is now ready for full-time ministry. This is the first time John, the Baptist and Jesus met face-to-face. When they met for the very first time, they were both in their mothers' wombs. I find it interesting that Elizabeth and Mary never allowed the cousins to meet in their younger years. Elizabeth knew Mary was carrying the Son of God, and I'm sure she would have told Zechariah about her experience when Mary came to visit. All the people of Israel were waiting for the Messiah to appear, but there's no mention in scripture that Elizabeth shared the news with anyone, maybe not even her husband. But I find it odd that Zechariah, as High Priest, would not have been aware that the Messiah was now on the scene.

It could also be that God prohibited them from revealing the identity of Jesus, after all, at that time, it would have been dangerous for Jesus to have the High Priest announce His arrival. It wouldn't be much longer before they were forced to flee Jerusalem to save His life. What is it that God is protecting us from when we are in our cave seasons? I have learned over the years that not everyone can handle the mysteries of God. I believe it's in the cave where we learn to steward the revelations given to us by our Father, and in this, our Father determines how much He can trust us.

"And Mary arose in those days, and went into the hill country with haste, into a city of Juda; And entered into the house of Zechariah, and saluted Elizabeth. And it came to pass, that, when Elizabeth heard the salutation of Mary, the babe leaped in her womb; and Elizabeth was filled with the Holy Ghost: And she spake, out with a loud voice, and said, Blessed, art thou among women, and blessed is the fruit of thy womb. And whence is this to me, that the mother of my Lord should come to me? For, lo, as soon as the voice of thy salutation sounded in mine ears, the babe leaped in my womb for joy. And blessed is she that believed: for there shall be a performance of those things which were told her from the Lord" (Luke 1:39-45).

Whether Jesus told His mother, Mary, that His time had fully come for full-time ministry is hard to say, but once Jesus stepped out in ministry, there was no turning back. Apparently, Jesus' family must not have understood who Jesus really was. It is surprising that Mary herself thought Jesus was going too far with His teachings. Maybe, the family was beginning to get the backlash from some of the things Jesus taught to the crowd. Jesus knew His time was limited and He had to do all that God sent Him to Earth to do. The Israelites were offended at the very thought that Jesus called God His Father. They knew Jesus was from Nazareth, His mother was Mary, His father was Joseph, and that His brothers and sisters lived among them. So, a lot of what Jesus taught them didn't make sense to them. How on Earth could He be so delusional to think that God was His Father? The crowd thought Jesus must have been demon-possessed; they couldn't see Him as anything other than an ordinary man from Nazareth, after all, they'd grown up with Him. How would you handle it if you suddenly became the manifested son of God that all of creation has been waiting for? What about your family? How would you convince them that you are no longer the person they have always known, and that God is now your Father?

But what about your family? I'm sure Jesus understood why the crowd would be offended by His teachings, but His mother and siblings? This makes me think His family had become so familiar with Him that they saw Him as a troublemaker like the rest of the Israelites. Also, there may have been questions among His brothers and sisters, wondering why He was getting so much attention. His family may have been getting some of the backlash from some of His teaching, since Jesus was getting so much attention from the large crowds that had begun to follow Him. At this point, there was such an uproar among the people and the religious leaders that the religious leaders started to make threats against His life. We know that Mary pondered the words she heard spoken concerning Jesus, but how did she think the fulfillment of those words was going to come about? At this point, she's had Jesus with her for thirty years. I'm sure she was caught off guard when Jesus began to stand up to the religious leaders. I can imagine memories of what was prophesied concerning Jesus' life began to flood Mary's soul. She had known peace up until this time, but now things were becoming tense and her concern for Jesus' safety were beginning to grow.

"Then the multitude came together again, so that they could not so much as eat bread. But when His own people heard *about this,* they went out to lay hold of Him, for they said, "He is out of His mind" (Mark 3:20-21).

"Then His brothers and His mother came, and standing outside they sent to Him, calling Him. And a multitude was sitting around Him; and they said to Him, 'Look, Your mother and Your brothers are outside seeking You.' But He answered them, saying, 'Who is My mother, or My brothers?' And He looked around in a circle at those who sat about Him, and said, 'Here are My mother and My brothers! For whoever does the will of God is My brother and My sister and mother'" (Mark 3:31-35).

Some of us can attest to the fact that winning your family's members can be one of the hardest fields to plow. Understandably, it may be quite difficult for them to believe the person they have known all their lives has somehow turned their life around. So, the waiting game begins. They know if they wait long enough, the old person will reappear and life will go back to normal. However, as they continue to look, if all they can see is the new person we have been transformed into, they will have to take note that we have been with Jesus. We have the greatest opportunity to evangelize our families simply by living a godly lifestyle before them, after all, they have seen us at our worst, but now, they get to see us in our transformed states. This doesn't mean that we won't stumble or occasionally fall. We just have to get up and keep going, knowing that we will eventually get there.

We can understand Jesus' stance when it came to His family. He was fully aware that He had to be about His Father's business. He could no longer just focus on His immediate family; His focus now must shift to the nation of Israel. The Word of God tells us that Jesus came to the lost sheep of the house of Israel. "But He answered and said, 'I was not sent except to the lost sheep of the house of Israel'" (Matthew 15:24). We know there are times when God will cause us to get away from our family and familiar surroundings so that God Himself can become our focus. Sometimes, God must transform our lives to such a degree that those who knew us can't help but take note that we have been with Jesus. At the same time, family can occasionally be a hindrance to your call. It can be difficult for them to see you beyond what they have always known about you. In those moments, don't allow anyone to keep you in an old place when God is calling you into the new thing He is doing in you.

We need to take note of everything that Jesus endured during His earthly walk, since the Word of God tells us that we are to be conformed into the image of Christ. This means there should be a constant renewal process going on in our lives. We shouldn't come to Christ and never see transformation take place. At some point in our walks with Him, we must recognize our need to relinquish anything that doesn't reflect who Christ is. I don't know about you, but I have a lot of work that remains to be done in me and I trust that He who has begun a good work in me will perform it until the day of Jesus Christ. This may take a little longer than we would like it to, but we trust that we will get there, and we will give our brothers and sisters the same grace to get there as well.

"If you knew, beyond the shadow of a doubt, that God was asking you to something, would you, do it?

160

What if He asked you to do something that might cost you your friendships, or your good reputation? What if He asked you to do something that seemed... completely nuts? Would you do it, no matter what the consequences were?

Mary and Joseph did.

If you go to Matthew 1:18-25, you can read about how Mary was pledged to marry Joseph, but before this, Mary became pregnant by the power of the Holy Spirit. It then tells about the angel who appears to Joseph in a dream, to reassure him about God's plan for their lives.

Now, that sounds neat and tidy, right? It's sometimes so easy to read scripture and forget how hard it must have been for Mary and Joseph to do God's will.

Put yourself in their shoes for just a minute.

What about Mary, having to convince her parents and Joseph that she's pregnant, not because she was unfaithful to Joseph, but rather by the Holy Spirit, because God chose her to give birth to the Messiah? As a parent, that might have been a hard tale to swallow. Think about your daughter coming to you with such a story! We know that Joseph was even contemplating quietly breaking the marriage agreement at this point!

Then we have Joseph, who is a righteous man within the community. There are only two possibilities. Either Joseph got Mary pregnant, meaning he will lose the perception of being a righteous man in their society, or Mary became pregnant by another, meaning she was guilty of adultery!

Nazareth wasn't a metropolis – I'm sure Mary had to deal with those dirty "looks" from neighbors, even as Jesus was growing as a young boy. Even today there are well-meaning people in the communities we live, who count the months between the wedding and the first baby!

Think about it. Would you be able to follow through with God's plan, if you lived during these times?

It goes without saying that what Joseph and Mary went through was a huge part in God's plan of redemption! They are more than just a "vessel" and "nice man who taught Jesus a craft". They put their lives on the line, even while Jesus was growing inside Mary's womb, to protect the Messiah.

What do we learn from Joseph and Mary? We can take away a lot from their lesson of obedience to God's calling. They saw that serving God and doing His will was far greater than being socially accepted."

Source: What We Learn from Mary and Joseph's Example by Jessica Wolstenholm

"Now unto him that is able to keep you from falling, and to present you faultless before the presence of his glory with exceeding joy, to the only wise God our Saviour, be glory and majesty, dominion, and power, both now and ever. Amen" (Jude 24-25).

God's Word says, "Brethren, if a man be overtaken in a fault, ye which are spiritual, restore such an one in the spirit of meekness; considering thyself, lest thou also be tempted" (Galatians 6:1). Our question remains—am I my brother's keeper? To the very end!

BACK TO THE GARDEN

Now that we have seen Jesus' earthly family dynamics, let's take a glimpse into His heavenly assignment. We know that from the Old Testament (Covenant) to the New Testament (Covenant), all prophecies pointed towards Jesus, from types and shadows to the actual fulfillment of scripture. Our mission is to find our way back to the Garden by locating God's plan of redemption that He set in motion when Adam and Eve fell.

Genesis: "Unto Adam also and to his wife did the LORD God make coats of skins and clothed them" (Genesis 3:21).

Exodus: "And the LORD said, I have surely seen the affliction of my people which are in Egypt, and have heard their cry by reason of their taskmasters; for I know their sorrows; and I am come down to deliver them out of the hand of the Egyptians, and to bring them up out of that land unto a good land and a large, unto a land flowing with milk and honey" (Exodus 3:7–8).

"Speak ye unto all the congregation of Israel, saying, In the tenth day of this month they shall take to them every man a lamb, according to the house of their fathers, a lamb for an house: Your lamb shall be without blemish, a male of the first year: ye shall take it out from the sheep, or from the goats: And ye shall keep it up until the fourteenth day of the same month: and the whole assembly of the congregation of Israel shall kill it in the evening. And they shall take of the blood and strike it on the two side posts and on the upper door post of the houses, wherein they shall eat it" (Exodus 12:3 -5-7).

"And the blood shall be to you for a token upon the houses where ye are: and when I see the blood, I will pass over you, and the plague shall not be upon you to destroy you, when I smite the land of Egypt. And this day shall be unto you for a memorial; and ye shall keep it a feast to the LORD throughout your generations; ye shall keep it a feast by an ordinance forever" (Exodus 12:13-14).

"In one house shall it be eaten; thou shalt not carry forth ought of the flesh abroad out of the house; neither shall ye break a bone thereof" (Exodus 12:46).

Leviticus: "And he slew *it*; and Moses took the blood and put *it* upon the horns of the altar roundabout with his finger, and purified the altar, and poured the blood at the bottom of the altar, and sanctified it, to make reconciliation upon it" (Leviticus 8:15).

"For the life of the flesh is in the blood: and I have given it to you upon the altar to make an atonement for your souls: for it is the blood that maketh an atonement for the soul" (Leviticus 17:11).

Numbers: He is the one who is lifted up in the wilderness of sin (Numbers 21:8-9) "And the LORD said unto Moses, Make thee a fiery serpent, and set it upon a pole: and it shall come to pass, that every one that is bitten, when he looketh upon it, shall live. And Moses made a serpent of brass, and put it upon a pole, and it came to pass, that if a serpent had bitten any man, when he beheld the serpent of brass, he lived."

Deuteronomy: "So they smote him, and his sons, and all his people, until there was none left him alive: and they possessed his land" (Numbers 21:35).

Joshua: He is the one who will lead the people into the land of rest (Joshua 1–2). "Now after the death of Moses the servant of the LORD it came to pass, that the LORD spake unto Joshua the son of Nun, Moses' minister, saying, Moses my servant is dead; now therefore arise, go over this Jordan, thou, and all this people, unto the land which I do give to them, even to the children of Israel."

Judges: He is God's appointed deliverer (Isaiah 61:1). "The Spirit of the Lord GOD *is* upon Me, Because the LORD has anointed Me To preach good tidings to the poor; He has sent Me to heal the brokenhearted, To proclaim liberty to the captives, And the opening of the prison to *those who are* bound."

Ruth: He is our kinsman redeemer (Ruth 4:1–10). "Then went Boaz up to the gate, and sat him down there: and, behold, the kinsman of whom Boaz spake came by; unto whom he said, Ho, such a one! turn aside, sit down here. And he turned aside and sat down. And he took ten men of the elders of the city, and said, Sit ye down here. And they sat down. And he said unto the kinsman, Naomi, that is come again out of the country of Moab, selleth a parcel of land, which was our brother Elimelech's: And I thought to advertise thee, saying, Buy it before the inhabitants, and before the elders of my people. If thou wilt redeem it, redeem it: but if thou wilt not redeem it, then tell me, that I may know: for there is none to redeem it beside thee; and I am after thee. And he said, I will redeem it. Then said Boaz, What day thou buyest the field of the hand of Naomi, thou must buy it also of Ruth the Moabitess, the wife of the dead, to raise up the name of the dead upon his inheritance. And the kinsman said, I cannot redeem it for myself, lest I mar mine own inheritance: redeem thou my right to thyself; for I cannot redeem it. Now this was the manner in former time in Israel concerning redeeming and concerning changing, for to confirm all things; a man plucked off his shoe and gave it to his neighbour: and this was a testimony in Israel. Therefore the kinsman said unto Boaz, Buy it for thee. So he drew off his shoe. And Boaz said unto the elders, and unto all the people, Ye are witnesses this day, that I have bought all that was Elimelech's, and all that was Chilion's and Mahlon's, of the hand of Naomi."

1 Samuel: He is God, rejected as the king (1 Samuel 8:7). "And the LORD said unto Samuel, Hearken unto the voice of the people in all that they say unto thee: for they have not rejected thee, but they have rejected me, that I should not reign over them."

2 Samuel: He is the heir of David's throne (2 Samuel 5:4). "David was thirty years old when he began to reign, and he reigned forty years."

1 Kings: He is the one who is greater than Solomon (Matthew 12:42). "The queen of the south shall rise up in the judgment with this generation, and shall condemn it: for she came from the uttermost parts of the earth to hear the wisdom of Solomon; and, behold, a greater than Solomon is here."

2 Kings: He is the one like Elijah, not accepted in his own country (Luke 4:24). "And he said, Verily I say unto you, No prophet is accepted in his own country."

1 Chronicles: He is the son of David (Matthew 22:41-46) "While the Pharisees were gathered together, Jesus asked them, Saying, What think ye of Christ? whose son is he? They say unto him, The son of David. He saith unto them, How then doth David in spirit call him Lord, saying, The LORD said unto my Lord, Sit thou on my right hand, till I make thine enemies thy footstool? If David then call him Lord, how is he his son? And no man was able to answer him a word, neither durst any man from that day forth ask him any more questions."

2 Chronicles: He is the only perfect king (1 Timothy 6:15). "Which He will manifest in His own time, *He who is* the blessed and only [a]Potentate, the King of kings and Lord of lords."

Ezra: He is the divine temple re-builder (Ezra 5;14-17 ; John 2:19). "But in the first year of Cyrus the king of Babylon the same king Cyrus made a decree to build this house of God. And the vessels also of gold and silver of the house of God, which Nebuchadnezzar took out of the temple that was in Jerusalem, and brought them into the temple of Babylon, those did Cyrus the king take out of the temple of Babylon, and they were delivered unto one, whose name was Sheshbazzar, whom he had made governor; and said unto him, Take, these vessels, go, carry them into the temple that is in Jerusalem, and let the house of God be builded in his place. Then came the same Sheshbazzar and laid the foundation of the house of God which is in Jerusalem: and since that time even until now hath it been in building, and yet it is not finished. Now therefore, if it seem good to the king, let there be search made in the king's treasure house, which is there at Babylon, whether it be so, that a decree was made of Cyrus the king to build this house of God at Jerusalem, and let the king send his pleasure to us concerning this matter" (Ezra 5:14-17).

"Jesus answered and said unto them, Destroy this temple, and in three days I will raise it up" (John 2:19).

Nehemiah: He is the guide of the remnant of God's people (Nehemiah 1:3; 2:5). "And they said unto me, The remnant that are left of the captivity there in the province are in great affliction and reproach: the wall of Jerusalem also is broken down, and the gates thereof are burned with fire" (Nehemiah 1:3). "And I said unto the king, If it please the king, and if thy servant have found favour in thy sight, that thou wouldest send me unto Judah, unto the city of my fathers' sepulchres, that I may build it" (Nehemiah 2:5).

Esther: He is our providential protector (Esther 4:14). "For if thou altogether holdest thy peace at this time, then shall there enlargement and deliverance arise to the Jews from another place; but thou and thy father's house shall be destroyed: and who knoweth whether thou art come to the kingdom for such a time as this?"

Job: He is our advocate to plead our case to God, and the redeemer (Job 9:33). "Neither is there any daysman betwixt us, that might lay his hand upon us both."

Psalm: He is the one who is crucified, but not left in Hades (Psalm 16:10). "For thou wilt not leave my soul in hell; neither wilt thou suffer thine Holy One to see corruption."

Proverbs: He is the wisdom of God, and the founder of the Earth (Proverbs 9:10). "The fear of the LORD is the beginning of wisdom: and the knowledge of the holy is understanding."

Ecclesiastes: He is the one who will bring everything into judgment (Ecclesiastes 12:14). "For God shall bring every work into judgment, with every secret thing, whether it be good, or whether it be evil."

Song Of Solomon: He is the best example we have of true love (1 John 4:10). "In this is love, not that we loved God, but that He loved us and sent His Son *to be* the propitiation for our sins."

Isaiah: He is the virgin-born suffering servant (Isaiah 7:14; Isaiah 53). "Therefore the Lord himself shall give you a sign; Behold, a virgin shall conceive, and bear a son, and shall call his name Immanuel."

God, speaking through His Prophet, Isaiah, said, "The people that walked in darkness have seen a great light: they that dwell in the land of the shadow of death, upon them hath the light shined" (Isaiah 9:2). "For unto us a child is born, unto us a son is given: and the government shall be upon his shoulder: and his name shall be called Wonderful, Counsellor, The mighty God, The everlasting Father, The Prince of Peace. Of the increase of his government and peace there shall be no end, upon the throne of David, and upon his kingdom, to order it, and to establish it with judgment and with justice from henceforth even forever. The zeal of the LORD of hosts will perform this. The Lord sent a word into Jacob, and it hath lighted upon Israel" (Isaiah 9:6-8).

Jeremiah: He is the branch (Jeremiah 23:5). "Behold, the days come, saith the LORD, that I will raise unto David a righteous Branch, and a King shall reign and prosper, and shall execute judgment and justice in the earth."

Lamentations: He is the man of sorrows who weeps over Jerusalem (John 11:35). "Jesus wept."

Ezekiel: He is God's servant and God's prince (Ezekiel 34:23-24). "And I will set up one shepherd over them, and he shall feed them, even my servant David; he shall feed them, and he shall be their shepherd. And I the Lord will be their God, and my servant David a prince among them; I the Lord have spoken it."

Daniel: He is king over the kingdom that will never be destroyed (Daniel 2:44). "And in the days of these kings shall the God of heaven set up a kingdom, which shall never be destroyed: and the kingdom shall not be left to other people, but it shall break in pieces and consume all these kingdoms, and it shall stand forever."

Hosea: He is the forgiving and redeeming husband to the unfaithful wife (Hosea 1:2). "The beginning of the word of the Lord by Hosea. And the Lord said to Hosea, Go, take unto thee a wife of whoredoms and children of whoredoms: for the land hath committed great whoredom, departing from the Lord."

Joel: He is the Savior of those who call on God (Joel 2:32). "And it shall come to pass, that whosoever shall call on the name of the Lord shall be delivered: for in mount Zion and in Jerusalem shall be deliverance, as the Lord hath said, and in the remnant whom the Lord shall call."

Amos: He is the rescuer of Judah (Luke 19:10). "For the Son of Man has come to seek and to save that which was lost."

Obadiah: He is the deliverer of Mount Zion (Obadiah 1:17). "But upon mount Zion shall be deliverance, and there shall be holiness; and the house of Jacob shall possess their possessions."

Jonah: He is the three days Jonah spent in the belly of the fish (Matthew 12:40). "For as Jonas was three days and three nights in the whale's belly; so shall the Son of man be three days and three nights in the heart of the Earth."

Micah: He is the blessing of Bethlehem (Micah 5:2). "But thou, Bethlehem Ephratah, though thou be little among the thousands of Judah, yet out of thee shall he come forth unto me that is to be ruler in Israel; whose goings forth have been from of old, from everlasting."

Nahum: He is the stronghold in the day of wrath (Nahum 1:7). "The LORD is good, a strong hold in the day of trouble; and he knoweth them that trust in him."

Habakkuk: He is the justifier of those who live by faith (Habakkuk 2:4). "Behold, his soul which is lifted up is not upright in him: but the just shall live by his faith."

Zephaniah: He is the channel through whom all nations can worship (Zephaniah 3:16-20). "In that day it shall be said to Jerusalem, Fear thou not: and to Zion, Let not thine hands be slack. The LORD thy God in the midst of thee is mighty; he will save, he will rejoice over thee with joy; he will rest in his love, he will joy over thee with singing. I will gather them that are sorrowful for the solemn assembly, who are of thee, to whom the reproach of it was a burden. Behold, at that time I will undo all that afflict thee: and I

174

will save her that halteth,and gather her that was driven out; and I will get them praise and fame in every land where they have been put to shame. At that time will I bring you again, even in the time that I gather you: for I will make you a name and a praise among all people of the Earth, when I turn back your captivity before your eyes, saith the Lord."

Haggai: He is the shaker of heaven and earth whose kingdom can never be shaken (Haggai 2:6). "For thus saith the Lord of hosts; Yet once, it is a little while, and I will shake the heavens, and the earth, and the sea, and the dry land."

Zechariah: He is the one betrayed for 30 pieces of silver (Zechariah 11:12-13). "And I said unto them, If ye think good, give me my price; and if not, forbear. So, they weighed for my price thirty pieces of silver. And the Lord said unto me, Cast it unto the potter: a goodly price that I was prised at of them. And I took the thirty pieces of silver and cast them to the potter in the house of the Lord."

Malachi: He is the one whose forerunner is Elijah (Malachi 4:5-6). "Behold, I will send you Elijah the prophet before the coming of the great and dreadful day of the Lord: And he shall turn the heart of the fathers to the children, and the heart of the children to their fathers, lest I come and smite the earth with a curse."

Matthew: He is the King of the Jews (Matthew 2:2). "Saying, "Where is He who has been born King of the Jews? For we have seen His star in the East and have come to worship Him."

Luke: He is the Son of Man, feeling what you feel. (Luke 6:5) ."And He said to them, 'The Son of Man is also Lord of the Sabbath.'"

John: He is the Son of God (John 20:30-31). "And truly Jesus did many other signs in the presence of His disciples, which are not written in this book; but these are written that you may believe that Jesus is the Christ, the Son of God, and that believing you may have life in His name."

Mark: He is the servant (Mark 10:45). "For even the Son of Man did not come to be served, but to serve, and to give His life a ransom for many."

Jesus in the Garden

Then they came to a place which was named Gethsemane; and He said to His disciples, "Sit here while I pray." And He took Peter, James, and John with Him, and He began to be troubled and deeply distressed. Then He said to them, "My soul is exceedingly sorrowful, *even* to death. Stay here and watch." He went a little farther, and fell on the ground, and prayed that if it were possible, the hour might pass from Him. And He said, "Abba, Father, all things *are* possible for You. Take this cup away from Me; nevertheless, not what I will, but what You *will*." Then He came and found them sleeping, and said to

Peter, "Simon, are you sleeping? Could you not watch one hour? Watch and pray, lest you enter into temptation. The spirit indeed is willing, but the flesh *is* weak." Again He went away and prayed and spoke the same words. And when He returned, He found them asleep again, for their eyes were heavy; and they did not know what to answer Him.

Then He came the third time and said to them, "Are you still sleeping and resting? It is enough! The hour has come; behold, the Son of Man is being betrayed into the hands of sinners. Rise, let us be going. See, My betrayer is at hand" (Mark 14:32–42).

They brought Jesus to the place called Golgotha (which means "the place of the skull"). Then they offered him wine mixed with myrrh, but he did not take it. And they crucified him. Dividing up his clothes, they cast lots to see what each would get. It was nine in the morning when they crucified him. The written notice of the charge against him read: THE KING OF THE JEWS. They crucified two rebels with him, one on his right and one on his left. Those who passed by hurled insults at him, shaking their heads and saying, "So! You who are going to destroy the temple and build it in three days, come down from the cross and save yourself!" In the same way the chief priests and the teachers of the law mocked him among themselves. "He saved others," they said, "but he can't save himself! Let this Messiah, this king of Israel, come down now from the cross, that we may see and believe." Those crucified with him also heaped insults on him. At noon, darkness came

over the whole land until three in the afternoon. And at three in the afternoon Jesus cried out in a loud voice, *"Eloi, Eloi, lema sabachthani?"* (which means "My God, my God, why have you forsaken me?"). When some of those standing near heard this, they said, "Listen, he's calling Elijah."
Someone ran, filled a sponge with wine vinegar, put it on a staff, and offered it to Jesus to drink. "Now leave him alone. Let's see if Elijah comes to take him down," he said. With a loud cry, Jesus breathed his last."
The curtain of the temple was torn in two from top to bottom. And when the centurion, who stood there in front of Jesus, saw how he died, he said, "Surely this man was the Son of God!" (Matthew 27:32-54).

"After this, Jesus, knowing that all things were now accomplished, that the Scripture might be fulfilled, said, "I thirst!" Now a vessel full of sour wine was sitting there; and they filled a sponge with sour wine, put *it* on hyssop, and put *it* to His mouth. So when Jesus had received the sour wine, He said, "It is finished!" And bowing His head, He gave up His spirit" (John 19:28-30).

"And these signs will accompany those who believe: In my name they will drive out demons; they will speak in new tongues; they will pick up snakes with their hands; and when they drink deadly poison, it will not hurt them at all; they will place their hands on sick people, and they will get well." After the Lord Jesus had spoken to them, he was taken up into heaven and he sat at the right hand of God. Then the disciples went out and preached everywhere, and the Lord worked with them and confirmed his word by the signs that accompanied it" (Mark 16:17–20).

Jesus Baptized by John

"Then cometh Jesus from Galilee to Jordan unto John, to be baptized of him. But John forbad him, saying, I have need to be baptized of thee, and comest thou to me? And Jesus answering said unto him, Suffer it to be so now: for thus it becometh us to fulfil all righteousness. Then he suffered him. And Jesus, when he was baptized, went up straightway out of the water: and, lo, the heavens were opened unto him, and he saw the Spirit of God descending like a dove, and lighting upon him: And lo a voice from heaven, saying, This is my beloved Son, in whom I am well pleased" (Matthew 3:13–17).

Jesus Is Tested in the Wilderness

"Then was Jesus led up of the Spirit into the wilderness to be tempted of the devil. And when he had fasted forty days and forty nights, he was afterward an hungred. And when the tempter came to him, he said, If thou be the Son of God, command that these stones be made bread. But he answered and said, It is written, Man shall not live by bread alone, but by every word that proceedeth out of the mouth of God. Then the devil taketh him up into the holy city, and setteth him on a pinnacle of the temple, And saith unto him, If thou be the Son of God, cast thyself down: for it is written, He shall give his angels charge concerning thee: and in their hands they shall bear thee up, lest at any time thou dash thy foot against a stone.

Jesus said unto him, It is written again, Thou shalt not tempt the Lord thy God. Again, the devil taketh him up into an exceeding high mountain, and sheweth him all the kingdoms of the world, and the glory of them; And saith unto him, All these things will I give thee, if thou wilt fall down and worship me. Then saith Jesus unto him, Get thee hence, Satan: for it is written, Thou shalt worship the Lord thy God, and him only shalt thou serve. Then the devil leaveth him, and, behold, angels came and ministered unto him" (Matthew 4:1-11).

Jesus achieved what Adam and Eve should have achieved when the devil came to Him questioning the things of God.

Without the shedding of blood, there can be no remission of sin.

"Pilate saith unto them, What shall I do then with Jesus which is called Christ? They all say unto him, Let him be crucified. And the governor said, Why, what evil hath he done? But they cried out the more, saying, Let him be crucified. When Pilate saw that he could prevail nothing, but that rather a tumult was made, he took water, and washed his hands before the multitude, saying, I am innocent of the blood of this just person: see ye to it. Then answered all the people, and said, His blood be on us, and on our children. Then released he Barabbas unto them: and when he had scourged Jesus, he delivered him to be crucified" (Matthew 27:22-26).

Jesus Gives up the Ghost

"Jesus, when he had cried again with a loud voice, yielded up the ghost. And, behold, the veil of the temple was rent in twain from the top to the bottom; and the earth did quake, and the rocks rent;_And the graves were opened; and many bodies of the saints which slept arose,_And came out of the graves after his resurrection, and went into the holy city, and appeared unto many._Now when the centurion, and they that were with him, watching Jesus, saw the Earthquake, and those things that were done, they feared greatly, saying, Truly this was the Son of God" (Matthew 27:50-54).

The Burial of Jesus

"When the even was come, there came a rich man of Arimathaea, named Joseph, who also himself was Jesus' disciple: He went to Pilate, and begged the body of Jesus. Then Pilate commanded the body to be delivered. And when Joseph had taken the body, he wrapped it in a clean linen cloth, And laid it in his own new tomb, which he had hewn out in the rock: and he rolled a great stone to the door of the sepulchre, and departed" (Matthew 27:57-60).

I don't think we understand everything that transpired when Jesus went into Hades, since it was because of our sins that Jesus took upon Himself that He was unrecognizable to the enemy. It wasn't until the enemy realized that Jesus had no sin and that he had Jesus in Hades illegally. You can almost hear Jesus saying, Hath God said?" Once Jesus took back the keys, the enemy could no longer hold Jesus in hades, so where did He go?

The Resurrection of Jesus

"The first day of the week cometh Mary Magdalene early, when it was yet dark, unto the sepulchre, and seeth the stone taken away from the sepulchre. Then she runneth, and cometh to Simon Peter, and to the other disciple, whom Jesus loved, and saith unto them, They have taken away the LORD out of the sepulchre, and we know not where they have laid him. Peter therefore went forth, and that other disciple, and came to the sepulchre. So they ran both together: and the other disciple did outrun Peter, and came first to the sepulchre. And he stooping down, and looking in, saw the linen clothes lying; yet went he not in. Then cometh Simon Peter following him, and went into the sepulchre, and seeth the linen clothes lie, And the napkin, that was about his head, not lying with the linen clothes, but wrapped together in a place by itself. Then went in also that other disciple, which came first to the sepulchre, and he saw, and believed. For as yet they knew not the scripture, that he must rise again from the dead. Then the disciples went away again unto their own home. But Mary stood without at the sepulchre weeping: and as she wept, she stooped down, and looked into the sepulchre, And seeth two angels in white sitting, the one at the head, and the other at the feet, where the body of Jesus had lain. And they say unto her, Woman, why weepest thou? She saith unto them, Because they have taken away my LORD, and I know not where they have laid him. And when she had thus said, she turned herself back, and saw Jesus standing, and knew not that it was Jesus. Jesus saith unto her, Woman, why weepest thou? Whom seekest thou? She, supposing him to be the Gardener, saith unto him, Sir, if thou have borne him hence, tell me where thou hast laid him, and I will take him away. Jesus saith unto her, Mary. She turned herself, and saith unto him, Rabboni; which is to say, Master. Jesus saith unto her, Touch me not; for I am not yet ascended to my Father: but go to my brethren, and say unto my Father, and your Father; and to my God, and your God. Mary Magdalene came and told the disciples that she had seen the LORD, and that he had spoken these things unto her. Then the same day at evening, being the first day of the week, when the doors were shut where the disciples were assembled for fear of the Jews, came Jesus and stood in the midst, and saith unto them, Peace be unto you. And when he had so said, he shewed unto them his hands and his side. Then were the disciples glad, when they saw the LORD. Then said Jesus to them again, Peace be unto you: as my Father hath sent me, even so send I you. And when he had said this, he breathed on them, and saith unto them, Receive ye the Holy Ghost: Whose soever sins ye remit, they are remitted unto them; and whose soever sins ye retain, they are retained. But Thomas, one of the twelve, called Didymus, was not with them when Jesus came. The other disciples therefore said unto him, We have seen the LORD. But he said unto them, Except I shall see in his hands the print of the nails, and put my finger into the print of the nails, and thrust my hand into his side, I will not believe. And after eight days again his disciples were within, and Thomas with them: then came Jesus, the doors being shut, and stood in the midst, and said, Peace be unto you. Then saith he to Thomas, Reach hither thy finger, and behold my hands; and reach hither thy hand, and thrust it into my side: and be not faithless, but believing.

And Thomas answered and said unto him, My LORD and my God. Jesus saith unto him, Thomas, because thou hast seen me, thou hast believed: blessed are they that have not seen, and yet have believed. And many other signs truly did Jesus in the presence of his disciples, which are not written in this book: But these are written, that ye might believe that Jesus is the Christ, the Son of God; and that believing ye might have life through his name." (John 20:1–31).

God's plan to get His God man back to the Garden has finally come full circle, and now the God man has been restored to the original intent of the Creator. Satan thought he had moved the God man from the place God created for His God man. Satan couldn't wrap his mind around the fact that he could never outsmart God, and there was no way for him to win.

EPILOGUE
Resource Materials

In conclusion, as Kingdom citizens, what is our responsibility in the Earth?

God has given the Earth to man to rule with authority, dominion and bring the Kingdom of Heaven to Earth. In other words, we are called to be Ambassadors for Christ. "Now then, we are ambassadors for Christ, as though God were pleading through us: we implore *you* on Christ's behalf, be reconciled to God" (2 Corinthians 5:20).

Definition of Ambassador
A person of high rank employed by a government to represent it and transact its business at the seat of government of some other power. The earliest examples of ambassadors employed occur in (Numbers 20:14 ; 21:21 ; Judges 11:7-19) afterwards in that of the fraudulent Gibeonites, (Joshua 9:4) etc., and in the instances of civic strife mentioned (Judges 11:12) and Judges 20:12 Ambassadors are found to have been employed not only on occasions of hostile challenge or insolent menace, (1 Kings 20:2 1 Kings 20:6 ; 2 Kings 14:8) but of friendly compliment, of request for alliance or other aid, of submissive deprecation and of curious inquiry. (2 Kings 14:8 ; 16:7 ; 18:14 ; 2 Chronicles 32:31) Ministers are called ambassadors of Christ. Bible Dictionaries – Smith's Bible Dictionary – Ambassador

We were instructed in Matthew 28:19 to "go therefore and make disciples of all the nations, baptizing them in the name of the Father and of the Son and of the Holy Spirit." The truth of matter is we barely go into our neighborhoods, let alone the nations. I believe God is calling us back to our first love.

An interesting statement about believers can be found in 2 Corinthians 5:20. It says, "We are ambassadors for Christ, as though God is speaking (or presenting Himself) by us..." You probably never thought about yourself as being an ambassador before. It's a pretty important job, with good pay and excellent benefits.

What's an ambassador? An ambassador is one who is sent to represent one country or government to another. While in the other country, the ambassador presents and demonstrates all the best that his or her home country or government has to offer.

When you give your life to God, you become a member of the Kingdom of Heaven. The Bible says that we are, at that moment, "translated into the Kingdom of God's dear Son."

You're not just here for your own plans or interests, but you're representing Heaven to those around you. Matter of fact, you're the only real sample of Heaven most people will ever see. What they'll know about God working in peoples' lives, they'll get from watching YOUR life. Pretty scary? Maybe. On the other hand, it means you're not limited to YOUR resources, because you're not out there representing yourself. Since you're representing God's government and HIS abilities, you have access to all the best that He has to offer. Remember, your whole mission is to give people a sample of what it is to have God at work in a person's life.

That's what will make them want to get to know Him for themselves. They have to be able to tell that something different is going on in your life. Something that just doesn't take place in the lives of the average people. How do they know? For one, you TELL them! You let them know what's going on inside you and in your life! That's right! You let people into your life! You bring your family, friends and co-workers into your inner circle, and let them share your experiences, your hopes, dreams, successes and failures. You tell them about answers to prayer and God's goodness towards you. That's part of being an ambassador for Christ. Being an ambassador for Christ means learning, growing and getting to know the One you're representing, in addition to learning His ways. You're called on to do something unique and something incredibly hard; you're called to represent someone to people in a way that they want to get to know Him for themselves.

That's why they keep looking at your life and checking you out to see if you're really what you say you are. But guess what? That's good for you! It challenges you to remain prayed up and full of the Spirit. When you're prayed up and full of God's Spirit, you become a person who's not afraid to feel and not afraid to express what's going on inside you. Most people try so hard to keep from hurting; they try to harden their hearts so that nothing hurts. They do it so well that, not only does nothing hurt, but nothing helps anymore! By avoiding being hurt, they also can't feel hope, joy or love. They become stiff and zombie-like emotionally.

That's where you come in. You've been healed of that. You're not deadened to your friends, co-workers and family. You're no longer so caught up on the fast track that you take people for granted. No, you're incredibly alive, aware, caring and full of joy. Jesus said, "That My joy may be in you, and that your joy may be full" (John 15:11).

People need to know that Jesus heals broken hearts, softens hardened hearts and changes evil hearts. You are a living demonstration of that. You've discovered that you don't have to be afraid to love, care or be close to people.

When you were living for yourself and living just for the moment, you really didn't care about learning how the world works or how to get along with other people. Why SHOULD you? You were too preoccupied with figuring out yourself! But, as an ambassador for Christ, you know how important it is to get to learn how things work; what makes people tick.

As an ambassador for Christ, you will find yourself doing the right things instead of the wrong things. You will find yourself doing things in excellence, instead of slipshod and haphazardly. You believe right, speak right and act right. And then, things turn out right! That's just how it works.

Right thinking, speaking and doing bring about right results.

Doing the right things and doing them the right way is one of the ways God has designed to feed the joy in your life. It's a part of the process of caring. Doing things right is what you DO when you care about other people. And it brings happiness. You really do feel better when you know you've done your best.

As an ambassador for Christ, you're in the habit of doing your best. You're not trying to earn God's love. That's already taken care of. You do your best, because you're allowing Him to work in you and through you to represent Himself to people in a foreign land.

Like Him, you find yourself becoming a "giver" instead of a "taker". You're letting Him give through you to people who are so used to being taken advantage of that, at first, they can't believe you're for real. But that's part of the job we have here. We're not giving out of OUR resources, but out of God's resources in Heaven. Philippians 4:19 says, "My God (I like that, MY God) shall supply ALL your needs according to HIS RICHES in Glory…" He doesn't supply our needs according to our needs, but according to His riches! According to Heaven's standard!

There's peace and confidence that comes when you know that you don't represent yourself, but that you represent Christ in your situation. Romans 14:17 says, "The Kingdom of Heaven is righteousness, peace and joy in the Holy Ghost."

> "You know that you can't control a lot of the things that happen, you know you can't control other people's behavior, but you don't let it upset you anymore.
>
> What happens and what other people do, these aren't what direct your path. You're not guided by circumstances or by other people's opinions.
>
> You're guided by the course set by the Spirit of God and the Word. So, you get pleasure out of being able

to rise above your circumstances and responding in the Spirit when someone is "actin ugly", as my cousin in North Carolina says. God gives you the resiliency to bounce back when you're tripped or knocked down.

Last, there's a sense of satisfaction as an ambassador for making a difference. You're a person that's unique. God has given you a specific set of people to reach, help, and guide. There's a contribution that only YOU can make. People that only YOU can reach. If you don't say it, it won't get said. It's that simple.

We have a ministry of reconciliation. Of getting people to come back to God, through Jesus. Jesus said in John 20:21, "As my Father has sent me, even so, I send you."

What we let people know is that God can be known, can be experienced and He will bring GOOD into their lives, if they'll BELIEVE what He says in the Bible. Job 22:21 puts it like this: "Acquaint NOW thyself with Him and BE AT PEACE. Thereby, GOOD shall come unto thee!"

You're leaving the world a better place than you found it. *2 Corinthians 3:6* says, "He has made us able ministers of the New Testament. Not of the letter, but of the Spirit. For the letter killeth, but the Spirit gives life." People are better off for knowing you. *Proverbs 13:17* says, "A faithful ambassador is health!" You're leaving behind a legacy of changed lives, of people who have been touched by the Spirit of God on the inside of you.

Source: The Worship Center

Responsibilities of an Ambassador

"The primary responsibility of an ambassador is to accurately represent and advocate for their home country's goals while abroad. In order to do this, they have to be thoroughly acquainted with their country's and ruler's policies, thoughts, and which outcomes are favorable or unacceptable. Similarly, we have to have a full, working (that means practical and useful) knowledge of God's plan—what has brought us to this point in history, how He plans to accomplish His end goal, and what our role is and will be—in order to be effective ambassadors for God and Christ on Earth.

One important thing to remember is that up until the last several decades, ambassadors (much like military leaders) had to do their work almost completely isolated from their country and ruler. It is only since the mass adoption of the telephone that ambassadors have been able to (or had to, depending on your viewpoint) check in constantly with their country's government to receive directions and permission to make decisions. For thousands of years before that, ambassadors lived in a foreign country, isolated except for an occasional letter or visitor from their home, conversing with foreign governments, proposing treaties, and helping further diplomatic relationships between countries. This was a huge responsibility and made it especially crucial that they understood their missions, their ruler's desires, and goals, and how to achieve them.

Benjamin Franklin is an excellent example of this type of ambassador. What many people do not know is that the U.S. could never have won the Revolutionary War without his efforts as an ambassador to France. While letters traveling across the ocean took months to arrive and be responded to, Franklin pursued the course he had been sent to follow, that of bringing the French into the war on America's side. He couldn't just telephone up the Continental Congress to see what they thought—he had to already know what they would think and how to make it happen. This he did, gradually and diplomatically bringing France into a military alliance with the fledgling U.S. and later negotiating the Treaty of Paris. In doing so, he ultimately doomed the British to fight two costly wars at once, spreading them so thin that they couldn't defeat the little upstart country.

Likewise, God does not give us a script or dictate exact actions or conversations over the phone. Instead, He gives us a manual with a host of guidelines, examples, some hard-and-fast dos and don'ts, and tells us what our ultimate goal is (eternal life in His kingdom). He does not tell us every minute step we must take to get there and every trial we'll face along the way. He gives us His spirit, His laws and teachings, and then empowers us to live our lives and make our own choices. We can go to him and ask Him questions. Sometimes we'll get an immediate answer, but more often the answer is "look at the instruction manual."

This is why we must spend time reading the Bible, studying it and thinking about it, learning its nuances and connections. We must spend time in prayer with God so that the lines of communication are open and understandable. This way when a situation arises, a conversation reaches a critical point, or a decision must be made, we already have the clarity of purpose to know how to proceed. This training is especially important because not only are we currently ambassadors, but this role is preparing us for our future eternal position leading and ruling as kings and priests in God's kingdom.

Additionally, ambassadors are responsible for protecting and defending their fellow countrymen abroad—in our case, our brethren. Paul explains to the Philippians how they should be caring for each other:

> "...fulfill my joy by being like-minded, having the same love, of one accord of one mind. Let nothing be done through selfish ambition or conceit, but in lowliness of mind let each esteem others better than himself. Let each of you look out not only for his own interests, but also for the interests of others" (Phil. 2:2-4).

> Christ told His disciples that their love for one another would be an identifying characteristic to the world (John 13:35). This was why Paul so severely chastised various groups of the ekklesia when they were disputing, judging, showing partiality to the wealthy, taking each other to court, and otherwise treating each other with disrespect (Rom. 14-15, I Cor. 6, I Cor. 11). We must spend time with our fellow brethren, exhort each other through trials, help the widows and those who are alone, and constantly be developing the outgoing, action-oriented love (*agape*) of God.

> One interesting aspect of ambassadorship is that the embassy is considered property of the ambassador's home country. So, if you visit an American embassy in Paris, you are stepping onto

American soil when you walk in. As ambassadors for Christ, anyone who comes into contact with us should realize that they're dealing with something a little different. We should "reflect the glory of the Lord" and look "more like him as we are changed into his glorious image" (II Cor. 3:18 NLT). That doesn't mean that we're going around shoving our beliefs in others' faces, but rather when someone comes into contact with us they should be able to see and feel God in our dealings."
Source: The Signs of Spiritual Erosion

Characteristics of an Ambassador
"Ambassadors come from a wide variety of backgrounds with different personalities and upbringings, but there are a number of personality traits and character virtues that they must develop and refine in order to be successful. These characteristics are similar to those we must develop as current ambassadors for Christ in order to be equipped for our future roles in the kingdom.

A firm foundation is critical for an ambassador—he or she must be a strong leader, respected and trusted, passionate about their job, with a strong sense of patriotism for their home country. Our foundation is, likewise, of absolute importance. Without a solid foundation of God's law, His plan, and His purpose for us through repentance and baptism, we cannot succeed in our quest for the kingdom—our ultimate home country (Heb. 6:1). They also need to be well-educated about their home and host countries' history and current circumstances, able to understand potential obstacles, read situations and know the best course of action. Paul tells us we, too, must "walk circumspectly, not as fools but as wise, redeeming the time, because the days are evil...do not be unwise, but understand what the will of the Lord is" (Eph. 5:15).

One of the things ambassadors must always be conscious of is the fact that they are a minority in their host country (as God's people are in the world) and be able to relate to many different types of people (I Cor. 9:19-22). They must always be diplomatic, using tact, wisdom, and discretion to navigate a foreign country. As Christ's ambassadors, we must remember that we are not told to go around offending people left and right, even when we disagree with the way they're living their lives. If you look at Christ's example, the only people he strongly chastised and offended were people like the Pharisees who set themselves up as spiritual leaders and led the people astray. Christ was loving, conciliatory, and forgiving toward the tax collectors, prostitutes, cripples, and others looked down on by society.

Paul gives us a good rule of thumb to live by, saying, "Let no corrupt word proceed out of your mouth, but what is good for necessary edification, that it may impart grace to the hearers" (Eph. 4:29). In other words, a good ambassador (whether worldly or of Christ) knows when to speak, and that sometimes keeping your mouth shut is the wisest and most loving course. Just because something is true does not make it right. We're told our speech should be "with grace, seasoned with salt"—in other words, adding flavor and benefiting the hearer (Col. 4:16). We are to always be ready to give an answer, but an answer that is right not only in content but also in tone and communication for the audience.

Along with gracious and wise speech, ambassadors much have the ability to teach and lead others. For Christ's ambassadors, this is an incredibly important trait now but even more so in the kingdom, when we will be teaching and training the whole world. Paul tells Timothy, "A servant of the Lord must not quarrel but be gentle to all, able to teach, patient, in humility correcting those who are in opposition" (II Tim. 2:24).

The Bible gives us myriad qualities we should be cultivating to help us become better and more effective ambassadors for Christ. Paul in particular was fond of writing whole lists of character traits (Tit. 1:5-9, Tit. 1:5-9, I Tim. 3). These lists cover all sorts of ground, from self-control and patience to soundness of faith and gentleness, to very practical things such as being hospitable (of extreme importance to worldly ambassadors as well).

Finally, a good ambassador is entirely grounded in ethical and moral judgment because they are constantly facing situations that do not have black-and-white answers. The only way for Christ's ambassadors to be able to do this is to have God's spirit dwelling in them and be connected to Him 24/7. Solomon prayed for the same kind of discernment when he was anointed king of Israel, saying, "Therefore give to Your servant an understanding heart to judge Your people, that I may discern between good and evil" (I Kings 3:9). Centuries later, Paul wrote to Timothy that he must "be diligent to present yourself approved to God, a worker who does not need to be ashamed, rightly dividing the word of truth" (II Tim. 2:15). Our role in the kingdom will be ruling, leading, and judging the nations, and we have to be preparing for this in our physical lives today.

Are we becoming good ambassadors for Christ?

Many places in the Bible make clear that we are not to take part in this world's rebellion against God, but that we are to be His representatives here on Earth for the present. Peter wrote to the ekklesia, encouraging them:
"But you are a chosen generation, a royal priesthood, a holy nation, His own special people, that you may proclaim the praises of Him who called you out of darkness into His marvelous light, who once were not a people but are now the people of God, who had not obtained mercy but now have obtained mercy. Beloved, I beg you as sojourners and pilgrims [i.e., not citizens, not of this world/land], abstain from fleshly lusts which war against the soul" (I Pet. 2:9–11)

We are called to be strangers in this world—not to blend in, but proudly represent and advocate for our home country as well as we possibly can until it is time to dwell in our home country for eternity. Paul encouraged the scattered Hebrews with this thought:

> "These all died in faith, not having received the promises, but having seen them afar off were assured of them, embraced them and confessed that they were strangers and pilgrims on the Earth. For those who say such things declare plainly that they seek a homeland. And truly if they had called to mind that country from which they had come out, they would have had opportunity to return. But now they desire a better, that is a heavenly

country. Therefore, God is not ashamed to be called their God, for He has prepared a city for them" (Heb. 11:13–16)

Source: In Christian Living, New Testament, Topic Studies

Made in the USA
Columbia, SC
31 December 2022

75281335R00122